PRAISE

Ground of Your Own Choosing

Beverly Ryle has created an original handbook for workers of the 21st century that is beautifully written and very inspiring. She teaches you how to be the master of your own life and proactively and positively maneuver in the new workplace and win. By telling you the truth about how you can be your authentic self in the new marketplace and giving you detailed guidance of what to do and how to do it, this book will become a career classic. I will certainly be recommending it to clients and colleagues as a must read.

> —Gail McMeekin, President of Creative Success
> (www.creativesuccess.com), author of *The 12 Secrets of Highly*
> *Creative Women* and *The Power of Positive Choices*

The clarity and wisdom in this book are amazing. Beverly Ryle reframes the task of finding work in a practical way that fits current times and helps the reader to be optimistic, proactive, and even excited about it. Chapter Four, "Throw Out Your Resume and Stop Networking," is worth the price of the book in itself. *Ground of Your Own Choosing* will be highly valuable to career counselors, as well as individuals who want to be more entrepreneurial about their careers.

> —Edwin C. Nevis, Co-Founder and Board Chair, Gestalt International
> Study Center (www.gisc.org), author of *Organizational Consulting:*
> *A Gestalt Approach* and *Intentional Revolutions: A Seven-Point*
> *Strategy for Transforming Organizations.*

Beverly Ryle provides wise counsel in *Ground of Your Own Choosing* to all those searching for a meaningful and satisfying professional future. It is required reading for a joyful journey to a career of freedom, opportunity and fulfillment.

> —Joan Goldsmith, founder of Cambridge College
> (www.cambridgecollege.edu), author of *Learning to Lead: A Workbook*
> *on Becoming a Leader* (with Warren Bennis)

Beverly Ryle has written the new "bible" on finding and creating work in today's world. In *Ground of Your Own Choosing,* she makes a strong case for turning the traditional job-search approach on its head. Integrating many of the views of the masters of organizational psychology with her own experience as a career consultant, she combines personal growth, innovative thinking, and entrepreneurial techniques into a winning and hopeful strategy for creating work. Her book is easy (and fun) to read, with creative analogies, stories, and useful case studies. The book is perfect for the new graduate, for anyone transitioning in work by choice, or not, and for all those who wish to enrich their own professional experience and make it more meaningful.

— Molly Eldridge, Assistant Director, Cape Cod Institute
(www.cape.org)

Whatever your reason for being involved in job-search, you should read *Ground of Your Own Choosing* before you take another step. This thought-provoking book offers hope to those caught in the job-search maze, struggling valiantly and often futilely to get hired. It lays out a clear path to follow to identify your personal skills and work preferences and align yourself with people and organizations that need and want you! It turns the job search process upside down and inside out and will revolutionize your thinking about how you define and find work in the 21st century. This book should cause everyone who provides job search advice to reconsider what they are currently telling their clients. It points out what we already know—that traditional approaches no longer work for many job seekers—and lays out a fresh approach that does work. Whether you are a career changer, a stay-at-home mom considering a return to the business world, a new graduate, or a recently "outplaced" seasoned professional, *Ground of Your Own Choosing* will help you view the job search in a whole new way.

— Barbara Hyle, Senior Associate Director, Alumni and Graduate
Career Development, Bentley College (www.bentley.edu)

© Kay Ryle

About the Author

As a career counselor and business consultant, Beverly Ryle has been helping corporate professionals, business owners, and people-in-transition achieve their full potential for over twenty-five years. After an extensive career as a resume expert, career counselor and corporate outplacement consultant in Fairfield County, CT, where she worked with clients at every organizational level, she moved to Cape Cod where she maintains coaching relationships with individuals all over the U.S. and provides customized, individual career retreats for people who are ready to take charge of their professional future.

Her ability to guide clients through a professional development process is built upon expertise in transition, communications, and negotiations, as well as the best practices of leadership, marketing, and consultative sales. This integration of counseling and business disciplines has proven to be very effective in the work she does with individuals and groups. In addition to individual counseling she provides transition, leadership, and sales training to business organizations, and regularly delivers professional development seminars on both business and career topics.

Her credentials include: graduate education in business and career development; professional certification with William Bridges and Richard Bolles; training at the Cape Cod Institute (www.cape.org) with thought leaders such as Joan Goldsmith, Charles and Edith Seashore, Margaret Wheatley, and David Cooperrider; Leadership in the 21st Century and the Cape Cod Training Program at the Gestalt International Study Center (www.gisc.org).

GROUND
of your own
CHOOSING

Winning Strategies for
Finding & Creating Work

BEVERLY RYLE

Illustrations by Eloise Morley

SHANK PAINTER PUBLISHING • CAPE COD • MASSACHUSETTS

GROUND OF YOUR OWN CHOOSING

Cover photograph by Michael Kaal
(michaelkaalphotography.com)

Illustrations by Eloise Morley
(eloisemorley@earthlink.net)

Book Design by Gillian Drake

The text of this book is composed in ITC Galliard

Copyright © 2008 by Beverly Ryle

PUBLISHER'S CATALOGING-IN-PUBLICATION DATA

Ryle, Beverly.
  Ground of your own choosing : winning strategies for finding & creating work
/ Beverly Ryle; illustrations by Eloise Morley.

  p. : ill. ; cm.

  Includes bibliographical references and index.
  ISBN: 978-1-888959-45-1

1. Job hunting—Handbooks, manuals, etc. 2. Career changes—Handbooks, manuals, etc. 3. Vocational guidance—Handbooks, manuals, etc. I. Morley, Eloise. II. Title.

HF5382.7.R95 2008
650.14

ORDERING INFORMATION:
info@GroundOfYourOwnChoosing.com
508.240.0432

SHANK PAINTER PUBLISHING COMPANY
P.O. Box 720, North Eastham, MA 02651

PRINTED IN USA

Creativity is the manifestation of the self.
Carl Jung

To Michael
whose steadfast support
brought my creativity to fruition and
whose love emboldens my best self.

This process of a good life is not, I am convinced, a life for the faint-hearted. It involves the stretching and growing of becoming more and more of one's potentialities. It involves the courage to be. It means launching oneself fully into the stream of life. Yet the deeply exciting thing about human beings is that when the individual is inwardly free, he chooses as the good life this process of becoming.

Carl Rogers
On Becoming a Person

Contents

Preface

The greatest discovery of my generation is that human beings, by changing the inner attitudes of their minds, can change the outer aspects of their lives.

William James

Several years ago, I did a workshop for a group of Bentley College alumni. Right after we finished lunch, just before we started back again, someone expressed frustration with the inefficiency and wastefulness of traditional job-search practices, and I made the offhand remark, "If I had my way, people would throw out their resumes and stop networking."

An electric charge went through the room. Thirty business professionals, some a few years out of college, others farther along in their careers, all of them well-versed in traditional job-search, came alive. Somebody had actually said out loud what they instinctively knew, that trying to find work the way we currently go about it is unproductive, frustrating, humiliating, and often downright awful. A career expert was telling them that it was not only acceptable but also entirely appropriate for them to feel as they did, and it was as if they heaved a collective sigh of relief. "Maybe it's not us," they thought, "maybe it's the methods themselves that aren't working."

I wished I could have put aside the agenda I planned for the afternoon to pursue the subject with them. What I suspect would have happened is that they would have told me they follow traditional job-search practices because they don't know what else to do. Not being able to answer the question, "What do I do instead?" is the reason people looking for work keep doing the same things and expecting different, less disappointing results.

This book was written to answer that question.

Within the professional lifetime of a single generation, we have seen transformations in the *kind* of work we do, *how* we work, *where* we work, *how long* we work at one place, and even *why* we work. Yet despite changes in virtually everything having to do with work, we still go about trying to find and sustain it in the same old ways.

The Information Age we are living in has left both long-term job security and the job-search practices associated with it in the dust. We may long for the stability we had between the end of the Second World War and the mid-1980's, but the fact is that college-to-retirement employment with one company is as much a thing of the past as the mimeograph or the Dictaphone machines of the 1950's. Work security will be recreated, not by big corporations, but by us, the people who do the work. For that to happen, the methods for finding work will need to be updated to reflect the way work is being distributed now—to contracted experts, consultants, service vendors, free-agents, and people who think of themselves that way even if they are job-employed rather than self-employed.

What worked in the past isn't working now, but it takes people quite a while to figure that out. In the meantime they keep doing what was handed down to them even though it's ineffective and at times dangerous. This book is an invitation to break out of the pack and try something different.

Job-search as it has been traditionally practiced is a sales process based on leads, generating them (research, networking), responding to them (print ads, web postings, contacts), and trying to convert one of them into a sale (a job offer). There are plenty of manuals around which repeat this message, but this book is not one of them. So be forewarned. If you are looking for techniques of power networking, or tips on how to wow them in an interview, or 101 ways to tweak your resume or polish your elevator speech, you will be disappointed. In fact, you will find me protesting against *exclusive* reliance on these mainstays of traditional job-search throughout.

On the other hand, if you have already dutifully plowed through

14

enough instruction books on the subject of finding work to know that a simplistic, here-are-all-the-things-you-should-be-doing approach is not helpful, keep reading.

If the headlines about layoffs, dying industries, outsourcing, etc. make you feel like the earth is rumbling under your feet, and you don't understand what's happening or how it will affect you, then find a comfortable place to sit and read Chapters I, II and III.

If you don't believe it's really possible to throw out your resume and stop networking, check out Chapter IV.

If you're in a dark place professionally and can't see the light at the end of the tunnel, take a look at Chapter V.

If you want to discover a competitive edge that lies entirely within your grasp, see Chapter VI.

If you think you've tried everything, and none of it has worked, peruse Chapter VII.

If you're tired of being a job-beggar and want to find ways to even the playing field, turn to Chapter VIII.

If you have an inner aversion to the idea of having to sell yourself, read Chapter IX.

If professional self-care is a foreign concept, and you don't have a clue how to do it, go to Chapter X.

This book contains no quick fix, no magic key to open the door to the perfect job or the big account. Instead it offers something better—hope, not for a short-term solution, but for a more meaningful and rewarding professional future. The same changes that are rocking professional security as it has been traditionally defined also offer us the freedom to shape our work lives so we can contribute at our highest level, feel professionally fulfilled, meet our financial obligations, and live balanced, enjoyable lives.

The stories that appear in these pages are fictionalized accounts of factual events. Names, locations, situations, and in some cases sexes, have been changed, but every example I give (with the exception of those in Chapter II) is based on real things that have happened in the lives of people I have known personally or professionally.

CHAPTER I

Ground of Your Own Choosing

Lee extended his hand to their leader. "General Pickett,"
he said, "place your division in rear of this hill, and be
ready to repel the advance of the enemy should they follow
up their advantage." "General Lee," Pickett replied, tears
flowing down his face, "I have no division now . . . ."

Kent Masterson Brown
Retreat from Gettysburg

I've spent most of my professional life as a career counselor teaching job-search practices I no longer advocate. In the 1980's, I was a partner in a resume business in Stamford, Connecticut, that specialized in helping the upwardly mobile professionals in the corporate headquarters between New York and New Haven advance their careers. The resumes we produced back then were a significant improvement over the style currently in use, a flat, colorless listing of employers and dates. We approached the resume as a marketing tool and wrote it as if it were advertising copy. This was novel at the time, and our resumes generated excitement and got results. In those golden days, when jobs were relatively plentiful and many people were on the move career-wise, before every job posting brought hundreds, if not thousands, of responses, having one of our resumes was almost guaranteed to get you an interview.

Later, when I opened my own office in my hometown of Bethel, Connecticut, I devised a resume process that was rooted in the same marketing practices I used to develop my business, but the language

I was speaking and the skills I was teaching were exclusively directed toward helping my clients get the next job.

My reputation as a job-search expert grew, and I was invited to consult for an outplacement firm, which took me back to Stamford again. In the ten years since I left, there had been a sea-change. The first time I was there, I was writing resumes to help people move from one corporate headquarters to another. Now those tall glass-and-steel structures were being depopulated by wave after wave of layoffs, and I was there to help move them *out*. Much of the population I served consisted of people being laid off after twenty or more years with the same company. A lot of them hadn't looked for work since they graduated from college, and my mission was to provide them with a superior resume and teach them how to conduct an effective job-search.

As I stood in front of conference rooms full of job-search novices, what I wanted most of all was to get them up to speed as quickly as possible. I was there to give them a crash course in the tried-and-true methodology so they would know what to do and not feel so desperate. The tactics I was teaching represented the best thinking of the time, but as I saw more and more people competing for fewer jobs, I began to question whether they were enough.

One day I read a headline about major layoffs at that unshake-able—or so it was thought—citadel of job security, IBM, and I remember feeling a shock wave go through me. I wondered how it might affect my professional life, just as I imagine my parents wondered how their lives would be changed when they learned that the Japanese had bombed Pearl Harbor.

When the Human Resources executives I worked with began to abandon the paternalistic notion that the organization had a responsibility to take care of its employees and started talking about expecting *them* to manage their own careers and take the initiative in getting the education and training they needed, I began to realize that a dramatic shift that went far beyond the ups and downs of the business cycle was under way.

My moment of truth, however, came during a meeting with a client who had had a twenty-year career as a financial manager with a Fortune 500 company before being let go in an early round of downsizing. He had taken to heart everything I taught him and followed all my suggestions to the letter. His resume was well-written. He networked effectively and was diligent in his follow-up. He was doing everything right and getting nowhere. All I could think of to do was to encourage him to keep at it.

One day, as he was leaving my office after a session, he confided in me that he was worried that if he was out of work much longer his son wouldn't be able to stay on at the Ivy League university he was attending. This was very important to him because he felt the education his son was getting there would enable him to be recruited by a good company where he would have a secure future.

I felt as if I'd been punched in the stomach. Here was a man whose career had been abruptly cut short, and yet all he could think of was how much he wanted his son to be able to follow in his footsteps down a path that was being washed away. The old days of one company for life weren't coming back for either of them. I suddenly knew that what I was teaching belonged to an era in the history of work that was passing, but I didn't know what to do about it until I went to Gettysburg.

Looking Back from the High Ground

Virtually the entire Gettysburg battlefield is now a national park. My husband and I toured it first by car guided by an audiotape, and then we decided to revisit some of the sites by bicycle to get a closer look.

One of our stops was on Seminary Ridge, at the place where General Robert E. Lee rode out to meet three of his divisions, or what was left of them, in full retreat after their assault on the Union forces failed. We discovered that a wide path had been mowed through the tall grass allowing us to retrace the route of the ill-fated attack of July 3, 1863, known as Pickett's Charge. We got off our bikes and walked them in reverent silence up the gentle slope toward Cemetery Ridge.

The meadow was alive with the hum of summer insects. Wildflowers swayed gently in the breeze. I found it hard to believe that this peaceful landscape had been the scene of so much carnage—6500 killed and wounded in a little over an hour. It was even harder to believe that *anyone* would have had the courage to leave the safety of Spangler's Woods behind us and march across almost a mile of open field under murderous rifle and artillery fire. Yet 12,500 Confederates had made that choice. As we made our way toward the clump of trees which served as the focal point of the attack, I increasingly felt around me the presence of legions of men who had given their "last full measure of devotion."

When we reached the top and the zigzag in the stone wall known as The Angle, the high water mark of the Confederate attack, I turned to look back over the ground we had just covered and could see in my mind's eye wave after wave of men moving up the hill toward certain catastrophe. The sense of waste I felt was both palpable and strangely familiar.

I thought about the clients I served in my career counseling practice and as an outplacement consultant—they were under fire as well. Some were casualties of layoffs. Others had survived, but lived with the knowledge that their security was threatened.

At that moment, two parts of me, the lifelong student of history and the career professional, came together, and I understood that what had happened at Gettysburg in 1863, and what was happening to my clients now had something very important in common. In both cases, monumental change had made the old ways of doing things worse than useless, and the fact that no one seemed to realize it, or know what to do about it, was having tragic results. To understand why I made this connection, I need to provide a little historical background.

On both sides, the Civil War was fought much the same way. This is not surprising, given that so many of its commanders had studied under the same teachers at the United States Military Academy at West Point and later fought side by side in the Mexican War of 1847. The tactics of 1863 had been developed three-quarters of a century earlier during the Napoleonic era and were based on sending a large number of soldiers to attack a force armed with smoothbore muskets which had a range of only about 250 yards and little accuracy at any range. One Civil War veteran remarked that it required considerable skill to hit a barn door at fifty paces with one.

By the 1860's, however, technological advances in weaponry had made the smoothbore obsolete. The rifle used during the Civil War was five times more effective than the old smoothbore, and sending a horde of men against an entrenched position, a maneuver which had been so successful fourteen years earlier during the Mexican War, was now a recipe for disaster. Against weapons that could hit a target over half a mile away, the attackers would be cut down before they could get close enough to engage. The nature of warfare had undergone a radical change, and the defenders dug in at the top of a hill had a clear advantage over even the strongest attacking force. The massed infantry charge had become an exercise in futility, but in battle after battle Civil War commanders kept doing it. It was what they had been taught, and it was all they knew.

The insanity of continuing to do what isn't working because you don't know what else to do is the same, whether you're fighting a war or trying to find work. Like generals on horseback directing the action in safety from the rear, career professionals, me included, were actually contributing to the carnage by equipping our clients with outmoded, inadequate job-search practices. We were preparing them to fight the last war, not the one they were in. The resume-driven "tactics" I was passing on to my clients were a product of the past, and like the infantry charge of the Mexican War, they were effective—in their day. Revolutionary changes in the world of work, however, had made them obsolete, just like the old smoothbore musket.

In less competitive times, before a single job posting could bring a flood of applicants, an individual stood a reasonable chance of getting through to someone who had the authority to consider him. Now, thanks to technology, companies can collect thousands of resumes and effectively screen applicants out, the equivalent of "shooting them down" before they can "engage," i.e., get in the door and sell themselves in a face-to-face meeting. I could see a distressing similarity between the soldier charging an entrenched position and the jobseeker trying to get past Human Resources. For both, changing times had turned it into a losing battle.

At first, the awareness was painful because I could see no alternative, but it turned out to be ultimately beneficial since it marked the end of my reliance on the formulas I had been taught. My discomfort led me to embrace a period of learning and experimentation that resulted in an about-face in the way I conducted my own professional life and went about helping others conduct theirs.

As I thought more deeply about what happened at Gettysburg, I could see in it an analogy that provided both an explanation for failure and a model for success. The Union forces carried the day because they were alert enough and nimble enough to occupy the high ground and position themselves where they had the advantage. The Confederates lost because they didn't. The army that won was the one that fought on the ground of its own choosing. For me, the way forward was to teach others how to conduct their work-search from the ground of their own choosing.

Are You Fighting the Last War?

To achieve long-term work security today, it's not enough to be a foot-soldier. You will have to play the role of general as well. A* successful work-search requires a plan that includes strategic direction, tactical execution, and logistical support. Not feeling equal to the responsibilities of command and control doesn't relieve you of the necessity of shouldering them. Here are some signs of a lack of preparedness in strategy, tactics, and logistics that indicate you are "fighting the last war."

Strategy

Not knowing your position.
This usually shows up as an inability to identify the career patterns that have brought you to where you are right now. You can't figure out where you're going unless you can see clearly where you've been and how you got where you are. If you're oblivious to the things you've habitually done, both to enhance and to retard your forward movement, you won't be able to draw confidence from your victories or learn from your defeats. Santayana's famous statement, "Those who are ignorant of history are condemned to repeat its mistakes," holds true no less for individuals than for nations.

Not having clear objectives.
Many people set about implementing a work-search campaign before they've identified and prioritized what they really want. I recommend having two or three clearly defined areas of interest that match your values and skills before "taking the field." If you don't have them you need to do more "scouting."

Lack of leadership.
In this war, you can't just follow orders. You have to create your own rules of engagement. The equivalent of sitting in the trenches, i.e. waiting by the phone, isn't going to work. You have to make it happen.

Tactics

Poor morale.
In the last war it was all about who you knew. In this war it's about how well you know them. If you neglect to build strong, meaningful

relationships, your career will suffer. This sort of relationship-building is as different from traditional networking as the "band of brothers" who've experienced combat together is from a group of drinking buddies.

Failing to maintain discipline.
Effective generals know that good discipline is just as important between engagements as it is during action. Armies constantly drill to maintain good order, and so should you. If you're having trouble structuring the time you spend on professional development, it's probably because you're not applying the same business disciplines to it that you would to a work-related project.

Getting bogged down.
To have the kind of mobility "this war" requires, you will have to travel light, which means you can't carry the baggage of unresolved career issues from the past. "Off-loading" requires time and space to fully experience any loss you may have suffered.

Not taking the initiative.
Research is valuable as long as you remember that its purpose is solely to prepare you for a face-to-face meeting. Nothing happens without a meeting, and when you learn how to fight this war, you will be generating as many of them as you can handle. If you're not out of your chair and across the table from someone at least three times a week, you're not fully engaged.

Logistics

Inadequate support.
During your "scouting phase" you can probably go it alone, but when you settle into taking decisive action, you'll need to maintain regular contact with people with whom you can share the details of your campaign. It's also a good idea to keep a journal to check in

with yourself regularly, and it doesn't hurt to have places you can visit for sanctuary and renewal when you need it.

Poor communications.

Developing a corps of people you can count on to support your career objectives is only as effective as your communications with them. If you allow yourself to be cut off from your "supply line" you can't expect to prevail. Maintaining regular contact with key "support personnel" is essential.

The wrong equipment.

Posting a resume is the "last war" equivalent of cleaning a rifle or polishing brass. Exclusive reliance on the resume is a sign that you're acting like a foot-soldier instead of running the show from headquarters. If you're spending more than ten to twenty percent of your time chasing print or electronic job postings, if the main focus of your campaign is moving resumes around like pins on a map, you aren't likely to meet your objective.

CHAPTER 11

Everything Has Changed

It's time we found a new way to think and talk about work, for until we do, we'll see no hope for ourselves and our children. It's a completely doable task. The clues and signs are everywhere—in how people are actually finding wonderful work situations and in how innovative organizations are already getting work done. The bad news is that, like all large societal changes, it is requiring us to abandon the vehicles that got us this far and strike out on foot for a while. And that is a frightening prospect.

William Bridges
Creating You & Co.

Imagine a dining room after a holiday meal. The dishes have been cleared away, the grandchildren have gone outside to play, and three generations of a family are at the table, talking about their problems with work.

There is Bob Fusty, the patriarch of the family. He accepted a buyout package after thirty-five years with a large manufacturer. He thought he would have a comfortable, worry-free retirement and wouldn't have to be concerned about money for the rest of his life, but his former employer is experiencing financial troubles, and his pension has been cut by almost a third. He is faced with having to go back to work, at least part time, to make ends meet.

Bob's daughter, Julie Quondam, has worked in accounting at a mid-sized company for seventeen years. The company is struggling to keep up with global competition, and she is constantly being asked to learn new technologies and take on responsibilities outside her comfort zone. She is unhappy in her work and nervous about the company's future.

Julie's twenty-seven-year-old son, Tom, works for a small start-up company that has just been bought out by a larger firm headquartered on the other side of the country. The new owners plan to merge his company's operations with theirs, and in a few months Tom's job will be eliminated. This is not a new situation for Tom—in the six years he has been working, he has already changed jobs more times than his mother and grandfather put together.

The differences in the work lives between the oldest and the youngest of these family members are greater today than at any other time in history. As I noted in the preface, in the last fifty years, the *kind* of work we do, the *way* we do that work, *where* we work, *how long* we remain in one workplace, and even *why* we work have all been reshaped by the powerful forces of change we read about every day—technology, corporate downsizing, globalization, etc.

Bob was a *producer* of a tangible product. He ran his department of the plant with a clipboard and a typewriter. He worked for the same company in the same physical location his entire professional life.

Julie has spent her career providing a *service*. When she started out, accounting systems were mostly manual, but over the years she has been forced to become skilled with computer software. As her company has scrambled to stay alive, her responsibilities, her title, and even the physical location of her workplace have changed again and again.

Julie's son, Tom, is what Peter Drucker calls a *knowledge worker*. He is used to doing business around the world with a laptop and a Blackberry®, working from home, from a Starbuck's®, from the front seat of his car, anywhere. He considers himself lucky if he can stay in the same job for more than three years.

The progression of these three generations, from *producer*, to *service worker*, to knowledge worker, illustrates the sweeping changes that have taken place in the last half century. Yet even though the nature of work today is radically different from the way it was when Bob began his career in the 1950's, when it comes to looking for work, all three, Bob, Julie, and Tom, will use the same approach, the one Bob used when he started out.

Everything having to do with work has changed except how we go about getting it!

As they sit around the table over coffee, Bob talks about needing to blow the dust off his resume and get it out there again. He's been going to the library in the mornings and scanning the help-wanted ads of several newspapers.

Julie has her fingers crossed that her seniority, plus being well-liked and conscientious, will allow her to hang on until her youngest child gets through college, but just in case, she has been attending weekly networking meetings hoping to hook up with a job where everything stays the same and she can just do her work and be left alone.

Tom is sure that somewhere on one of the Internet career websites he frequents he will find a posting for a job that matches his qualifications, and he will be able to step right into it without missing a beat (or a car payment).

The differences in their methods are only on the surface. The underlying strategy is fundamentally the same. It's based on blind searches and chasing leads. This "sales" model of job-search is rapidly losing its effectiveness in the Information Age we live in, and yet Bob, Julie and Tom will follow it anyway, looking at ads (classified or Internet), sending out resumes, networking, running the gauntlet of the interview, waiting, not hearing back, getting rejected, and they will repeat the process *ad nauseum*. Traditional job-search remains embedded in the psyche of all three generations (and the vast majority of the U. S. working population) even though every other aspect of their work lives has undergone transformation.

Even Tom, who considers himself much too hip to listen to Bill

Haley or drive an Oldsmobile, has unconsciously adopted an anachronistic *modus operandi* handed down from his grandfather's generation. And the irony is that, even if his search is successful, it will only have gained him breathing space. It will not have made him any more confident or better prepared for the next time he is faced with having to look for work.

Traditional job-search was created in the placid lakes of long-term employment, not the rapids of constant change. Flat water isn't coming back, and yet people, even those who instinctively know this, keep paddling against the current. They persist in exerting tremendous effort at something which at best will allow them to stay in place, and at worst cause them to get hung up on the rocks or capsize. To navigate these choppy waters they will need to fundamentally change how they think about work by:

- Shifting their attention away from a dependence on others (employers) to themselves.

- Learning business development skills and managing their career as if it were a small business.

- Making the most of the competitive edge that comes with authenticity, knowing themselves well enough to clearly articulate their unique value in the marketplace.

- Practicing new ways of taking care of themselves professionally.

The Workquake

Bob, Julie and Tom, along with 40 percent or more of the workers in the U. S., are caught up in what economists and others who follow business trends call job churn, the movement of people into and out of the labor market. Job churn has always been with us, but over the last few decades it has grown significantly in size and scope.

Robert Kimmitt, Deputy Secretary of the Treasury, writing in *The Washington Post* (January 23, 2007, p. A17), has provided some telling statistics:

- The year 2006 saw the highest turnover rate since the government began keeping records on it in 2000.

- 55 million people left their jobs in 2005.

- Average job tenure has dropped to 6.6 years.

- Today's workers will have an average of ten different employers between the ages of 18 and 38.

"Unlike their grandparents, who built careers around companies rather than opportunities," Kimmitt writes, "members of the class of 2007 will enter the workforce with an understanding that change may be the only constant in their professional careers."

Statistics like these indicate something momentous, even earth-shaking, is happening, but they do little to shed light on the underlying causes. They are like a news report of a certain number of people killed, injured, and left homeless that fails to mention there was a hurricane.

This data is the surface manifestation of an upheaval that is going on at the core of how we define work. Like tectonic plates moving against each other along a fault line, the Industrial Age, where work was organized in discrete bundles directed toward production, is receding, while the Information Age, where work is organized around knowledge directed toward service, is advancing. The stress of these two forces moving in opposite directions has produced what thought-leaders are calling a "workquake," and the familiar structures of employment security have been swallowed up in the chasm it has left behind.

Jobs Haven't Been Around Forever . . .

Jobs are a product of the Industrial Revolution. Before that, people didn't work at a narrowly defined set of tasks for a specified number of hours a day. They had a great deal to do between sunrise and sunset, but they didn't think of it as a job, not the way we do. For them, work was simply a collection of self-initiated actions they performed on a regular basis in order to sustain their way of life.

In fact, the notion of a job was a hard sell in the early days of the industrial era. The farmers, merchants, and artisans of the early nineteenth century were what we would now call free agents, and to them, the idea of giving up their independence, craftsmanship and sense of community was absurd. They were so resistant that many industrialists turned to recruiting young unmarried women for their factories and made accommodations for them so that their families would allow them to leave home to work.

In one of the great ironies of history, the pendulum has swung back the other way, and now two hundred years later, we are just as reluctant to embrace free agency as the pre-Industrial Revolution workers were jobs. The process of change is just as bewildering to us as it was to them. Being human, we want to cling to the familiar, even as we watch it being replaced before our eyes.

. . . and Now They're Disappearing

Jobs as we have known them are disappearing, not just in ways we are acutely aware of, such as when the voice on the other end of the telephone line has a foreign accent or is computer-generated, but at a much deeper level. In the Information Age, it isn't necessary for physical and human resources to come together in the same place for work to get done. Much of it can be done as well or better by people who are electronically connected. This makes it possible, as in the pre-Industrial Revolution days, for work to take the shape of a collection of tasks rather than a nine-to-five, Monday-to-Friday routine.

Like the mills and factories of a bygone era, the large corporate headquarters is becoming a thing of the past as the work that goes on there is being done less and less by people with "jobs" and increasingly by people who can do it well and cost-effectively from anywhere as independent contractors or small business owners.

Just as all rivers flow to the sea, all jobs are being judged by employers according to how they affect the bottom line. Faced with unprecedented competitive challenges, they are looking at their employees through a different lens. They want to know how each contributes to revenue generation, and they believe it is the employee's responsibility to demonstrate that he is able to add value to the organization.

This would appear to increase the dominance of the employer, but the fact is, the employer-employee relationship is changing on both sides. While employers are redefining their terms of engagement, workers are making their own decisions about where they want to put their energy and how they want to commit themselves. In sectors where there has been a high demand for talent, the shift from company loyalty to career self-interest has been relatively painless. In other cases, the transition has not been so gentle, and job loss, actual or the fear of it, has generated a sense of victimization and isolation. Many workers are having a hard time seeing what is happening to them in context.

If Bob, Julie and Tom, were able to look beyond their own misfortune—like when the power goes and you step outside to see if the rest of the lights on your street are out too—they would see it's not just them. Everyone has been affected. They would understand that what they are experiencing is the aftermath of the workquake.

The chasm is a reality. The only question is whether it will inspire a resolve to meet the challenge it presents or instill a sense of defeat. The mission of every person seeking work in the drastically changed professional landscape of the 21st century will be to find a way across the divide.

Dealing With The Aftermath

Those who have yet to be touched directly by the workquake pretend that the chasm doesn't exist. They don't want to acknowledge that any change has taken place. They prefer to believe they can operate as if it's business as usual.

Julie Quondam knows she's not as adept at using technology as her younger co-workers, but she puts on a brave front and tries not to think about it. Instead of taking the initiative to get the training she needs to make her more comfortable and productive, she  fantasizes that she'll be able to get by as she always has by exchanging loyalty and dedication for being taken care of by her employer. Julie is in denial.

Those who have experienced being out of work have first-hand knowledge of the chasm. Rather than think about its effect on their future, however, they focus their energy on trying to find another job just like the one they lost, or, if they have managed to survive a layoff, holding on to the one they have at all costs.

Tom Quondam fell into technical sales because it was a bird in the hand and paid enough for him to get married. He's only been in the field for a few years, but already he feels trapped. He doesn't like what he's doing all that much, and most of his jobs have been lateral moves made with no clear sense of direction. He really misses the energy he had when he helped manage an electronics store for a couple of years after college, but he uses the justification that he has a new family to support to shut down the inner nudge that invites him to explore these feelings. He is clinging to the edge.

Finally there are those who found the earth opening up under their feet—the embittered corporate professional who's been laid off and can't find work at a comparable level; the business owner who has been driven under by global competition or changes in technology; the college graduate who has discovered that the profession she prepared to enter is oversaturated; the retiree who has had to go back to work because he can't make it on a fixed  income. Those who have had their professional lives turned upside down are the most severe casualties of the workquake. They have the right to grieve their loss, but they also need to make a decision, after an appropriate period of mourning, to move on. If they don't, they will end up in freefall.

Bob Fusty worked hard his whole life, and feels that it's unfair that he should have to go back to work at his age. He sees few if any possibilities outside of the kind of work he was doing before he retired, and yet he doesn't see how he could possibly go back to it. Even if he were physically able, he can't imagine anyone would want him. But he can't think of anything else, and this has left him feeling paralyzed. He makes sarcastic remarks in a loud, angry voice and blames everyone from the people who run his former company all the way up to Congress and the President for his predicament.

Brave Souls

There are a few brave souls who have the courage to look hopefully across the divide. They don't know (yet) how they're going to get over to the other side where the professional security they envision lies, but they are ready and willing to take responsibility for discovering new ways to move forward.

Where those who are in denial, clinging or in freefall see only an impassable abyss, they see an opportunity to build a bridge to a better way of life. They know that developing alternative approaches to finding work is a major endeavor, yet they also know that when the changes in the workplace run deeper than the ebb and flow of employment trends, they must deepen their response to them. They understand that business as usual will not get them where they need to go. They will need to stretch themselves to accommodate a new outlook that fundamentally changes how they think about work.

As the discussion about work around the table at the Fusty household begins to wind down, and they're getting out the Scrabble® game, Julie's younger sister Jane Harbinger, who has been helping her mother in the kitchen, rejoins them.

Hers is a very different story. A year ago, her corporate career was sailing along nicely. Then a major reorganization left her saddled with a set of responsibilities that no longer matched her talents or her interests.

Her initial response was the same as the rest of her family—polish up the resume, answer the ads, etc. But after a while, when her instincts told her she wasn't getting anywhere, she began to look for another course of action.

When it was suggested to her that she needed to look at the bigger picture of managing her career, not just the immediate concern of getting another job, she began to think about how she might take charge of her own professional future.

When she was told that managing her career would have a lot in common with owning a business, she realized she needed entrepreneurial skills and enrolled in a business development program. One of the requirements of the program was to write a business plan, and Jane decided to adapt the assignment to her own situation by creating what she called a "career business plan." As she was working on it, she found she had trouble articulating the features and benefits of her product—herself—nor did she know what she was ideally suited for. This led to an intense period of self-discovery which continued until she was able to integrate her skills and interests into a set of clearly focused professional goals.

At the same time that she was learning about business ownership and herself, she systematically began to build a infrastructure of support by reconnecting with professional peers she had lost contact with and by regularly communicating with people whose professional wisdom she valued.

It reminded her of when she decided to look for an alternative treatment for her allergies. She didn't like being dependent on the medication that had been prescribed by her doctor. It wasn't doing much for her, plus it had unpleasant side-effects. She found a naturopath who started her on a regimen which required her to make major changes in her lifestyle. She had to find out about nutrition, avoid certain foods, and learn to like new ones that she would never have tried otherwise. It had taken time, but the result was a lasting remedy rather than temporary, sporadic relief.

She could see that, like alternative medicine, the Ground Of Your Own Choosing approach to finding work would not offer the quick fix promised by traditional job-search (a promise that is often illusory), but she was attracted by the prospect of creating long-term security for herself, even in the midst of upheaval. She decided to take the plunge and change how she thought about work, just as she had changed how she thought about her health.

After a year of putting into practice what she has learned, she has a new platform for professional security, and the view from it is very different from the one her father, sister, and nephew have.

Jane now sees the people she works for not as employers but as *clients*, and herself not as an employee but a *vendor* who provides services to them. She knows it's not a good idea for her to think about relying on a single source of work. Like any business, she needs to be constantly scanning the horizon for new opportunities. And finally, she realizes that it's not enough for her to be managing her career only when she enters the troubled waters of job churn. She needs to be working at it all the time by treating it as if it were a small business and developing the skills that will make her comfortable running it.

Jane is now able to see what she does as a collection of "chunks of work" performed for different people, under different conditions, at different times, in different locations. She recognizes that her work can take a wide variety of forms—a long-term contract (formerly known as a job), short-term projects, consulting arrangements, collaborative partnerships, freelance assignments.

Having freed herself from thinking of work narrowly, she is able to do more than just endure the pain of the seismic shift that is under way. She is ready to seize the opportunities that come with new forms of work that offer advantages few jobs can—autonomy, personal fulfillment, and even long-term security.

CHAPTER III

Jobthink

Successful careers are not "planned." They are the careers
of people prepared for the opportunity because they know
their strengths, the way they work and their values. For
knowing where one belongs makes ordinary people—hard-
working, competent but mediocre otherwise—into out-
standing performers.

> Peter Drucker
> *Management Challenges*
> *for the 21st Century*

The average person who buys a lottery ticket has few illusions about what he's doing. If he doesn't already know he's seven times more likely to be struck by lightning than to win the jackpot, he at least understands that the odds are pretty long. Yet he does it anyway, because there's a part of him that wants to be *set for life,* and he's willing to gamble, even if the chances are slim.

Similarly, the person who sends out a resume in answer to an Internet posting or a blind ad is probably aware that there are hundreds, possibly thousands, of others applying for the same position, but like the guy with a Powerball ticket in hand, he's thinking, "Hey, you never know."

Lottery advertisements claim, "All you need is a dollar and a dream." The unspoken but widely believed job-search equivalent is, "All you need is a resume and a dream." The dream is that somewhere there exists a position which will fit your interests and skills like a glove, relieve all your financial concerns, and consistently deliver a high level of

43

satisfaction. It's out there somewhere, waiting, if you can only find it.

But what if jobs aren't able to provide those things any more (assuming they ever did)? What if the workquake has made it impossible for jobs to make good on that promise?

Chasing the things that jobs are no longer able to offer is what I call *jobthink*. Jobthink has two important things in common with playing the lottery—the odds, obviously, and the motivation. People play the lottery in the hope of winning so they'll never have to work again. Jobthinkers live in the hope of finding the perfect job so they'll never have to *look* for work again. They want to be exempt from the fear, uncertainty, and confusion which goes with being in transition.

Jobthinkers know this doesn't happen very often, that job churn is as much a reality as the canister of losing scratch tickets beside the cash register at the convenience store, yet they still go on, in acts of quiet desperation, posting and hoping maybe next time they'll be a winner. They invest a lot of time and energy in an area where there is very little probability of success, and in doing so they exercise a subtle form of sabotage on themselves. By placing their hopes on an unrealistic dream, they abdicate their responsibility for creating work and undermine their ability to take ownership of their professional life.

Descent Into Entitlement

The jobthinker puts himself in a position where there is very little he can do to advance his cause. No matter what action he takes, he ends up waiting for a response. Long periods of downtime and one-sided conversations with no resolve are difficult for anyone, but they are particularly hard for people who have chosen to invest so much of themselves in a "resume and a dream." Waiting, without being able to do anything to expedite the outcome, leads to frustration, even in the most determined or the most patient. Over time, frustration builds to resentment, eventually culminating in outrage, a protracted and intensified version of what happens inside you when you're stranded in an airport for an indeterminate period of time.

The downward spiral into negativity is very dangerous for someone looking for work because his capacity to be positive about his abilities and confident about the contribution he can make is essential to his marketability. He can try to hide the negativity from others, but he can't hide it from himself. Ultimately it will corrode his conviction in the value of what he has to offer, himself, and there are very few of us who can be effective at selling something we don't wholeheartedly believe in.

Even before jobs started falling into the chasm created by the workquake, job-search practices were challenging. Now, however, with the odds against success steadily increasing, the jobthinker who relies on them is very likely to get caught up in an internal monologue that goes something like, "I want a job, I need a job, I *deserve* a job." When he gets to "deserve" he's in real trouble, because the belief that you deserve something you're not getting is a slippery slope to feeling like a victim. Even if he doesn't go that far, if he sees himself as needy, so will others, and being seen as needy is totally incompatible with being thought of as a valuable resource.

A few years ago, the members of a support group for people out of work formed in response to massive layoffs in an urban area took an action which demonstrated that they had crossed the threshold to victim-hood. They began to gather at a subway station during morning rush hour, handing out resumes to people on their way to work like political activists passing out flyers or street evangelists handing out religious tracts.

These were white-collar professionals who had gone to good colleges, advanced up the corporate ladder, conducted their job-search just as they had been told, and yet there they were, quite literally out on the streets. The statement they were making came from a deep sense of entitlement, the conviction that they *deserved* to be hired. We can understand the anger and the frustration of these workquake "refugees," but if they don't find constructive ways of dealing with their outrage, it will take them to the bottom of a dark hole which will be difficult to climb out of.

The case of Barbara Ehrenreich offers a striking example of this descent. Ehrenreich is a journalist who first gained national attention as the author of *Nickel and Dimed: On (Not) Getting By in America* in which she wrote about her experiences impersonating a low-skilled worker in various minimum wage jobs. Her next book, *Bait and Switch: The (Futile) Pursuit of the American Dream*, is the result of another undercover operation, this time posing as a middle-class professional trying to find a job in corporate America. By the end of her investigation, in which she has done everything right, according to the rules of traditional job-search, she still has not found a job and has no hope of finding one. She has not even gotten a real interview. From this she concludes that the middle-class has been sold a bill of goods. They are victims of fraud—hence the title, *Bait and Switch.*

It's ironic that, without being in the least aware of it, Ehrenreich ends up demonstrating something altogether different from the foregone conclusion she sets out to prove. What her experiences actually expose is the "futility," not of the American Dream, but of traditional job-search. Over the course of her ten-month "experiment" trying to pass herself off as a corporate job-beggar, she endures an assortment of career charlatans, pays a "peppy coach" to become a "pseudo-boss" she can practice with, tweaks her resume endlessly, goes to countless demeaning networking meetings, dons the corporate "uniform," a tan suit with soft lapels that make her more "approachable," according to the image consultant she hired, and does a host of other things that turn out to be equally useless. Never once does it occur to her that all these things are relics of the Industrial Age which don't work in the Information Age.

She becomes a sheep following the herd from one bad experience to the next. She puts herself out there again and again to get shot down, and the result is as predictable as the slaughter on the third day at Gettysburg.

Her story is a catalogue of actions that go nowhere, and yet the list of things that she does *not* do to help herself is staggering. She doesn't listen to her gut when it tells her that some of the actions she has been advised to take won't work, or that some of the people who claim to be able to help her are incompetent or untrustworthy. She instinctively knows that she would benefit from a support system of spontaneous, genuine connections, yet she chooses to attend orchestrated, superficial networking sessions instead. She makes no effort to see what is happening to her in the context of fundamental changes in the world of work that have nothing to do with corporate callousness. She doesn't use her natural gifts and talents as a researcher and writer. She isolates herself and never asks for help from the people she has established professional relationships with. She isn't interested in thinking like an entrepreneur or learning business development skills. She doesn't entertain the possibility that a period of uncertainty and confusion can be a creative space for renewal, or that transition is not a euphemism for being out of work but a source of genuine wisdom encouraging her to take a long, hard look at the patterns that need to end in herself, starting with the sour, entitled attitude she broadcasts a mile off.

Instead, she throws up her hands and says, "If there were other, entirely different, tacks to take, none of the job seekers I met seemed to know them." In the end she returns to her career as a journalist and author and leaves her fellow jobseekers on the battlefield, fighting for a cause she has declared lost.

Limited Access

For jobthinkers, looking for work is virtually synonymous with putting together a resume. Yet by relying on a resume, the jobthinker limits his access to work to a single point of entry, the published job market. He positions

himself on the outside of an organization, trying to get in, and closes himself off to opportunities that may not come packaged as a nine-to-five job. *He wants something from the organization*—a paycheck, benefits, and especially, long-term security.

The vendor/service provider, on the other hand, positions himself within the wider circle the organization draws upon for the resources necessary for its day-to-day operations and vital to its growth. He sees himself as someone who has *something of value to offer the organization.*

A jobthinker's only access is down a one-way, heavily-traveled thoroughfare leading to a single point of entry, Human Resources. There the conversation is not with people inside the organization who have work that needs doing and problems that need solving, but with gatekeepers whose function is to block entry by screening out applicants.

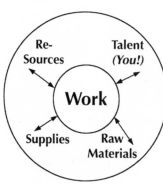

Vendor/service providers are able to take advantage of multiple entry points. They travel a system of broad highways which connects them directly to the people in the organization who need help.

The activities a jobthinker engages in are classified under the heading of employment practices which reside at the administrative core of a company. These practices are characterized by entrenched policies, rigid procedures, and innumerable hoops to jump through. The exchange between the jobthinker and the prospective employer is governed by non-negotiable protocols, and the conversation is *person-to-business*, between the small and powerless and the large and powerful.

Vendor selection is a *business-to-business* dialogue which takes place where the membrane separating the organization from its needed resources is permeable and there is much more parity, flexibility and

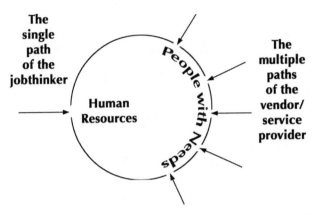

openness. The conversation is between peers who within the context of the work at hand have equal power to negotiate arrangements that are mutually beneficial.

The jobthinker is attracted to classified ads, Internet postings, recruiters, etc. because they offer the possibility of a ready-made work opportunity he can step right into. He doesn't have to do what the vendor/service provider does, which is to create work opportunities for himself. It's natural that this would be appealing, but there is a downside. Assuming the jobthinker gets hired, will the job match his skills, interests and personality? Based on nothing more than a little research and a couple of interviews, the likelihood of an ideal fit is small. It depends upon the luck of the draw.

It has long been known that 20 percent or less of people looking for work find it through the published job market, while 80 percent or more find it through the connections they have with people in their professional circles—and by this I mean *genuine*, reciprocal relationships, not the superficial kind that come from traditional networking (more on the difference in Chapter IV). Yet 100 percent of the energy of the jobthinker is directed toward the 20 percent of the pie, the published job market.

If we wanted to diagram what all the work that needs to be done within an organization looks like, we might draw a triangle to represent an iceberg, with a wavy line to indicate the water line and show

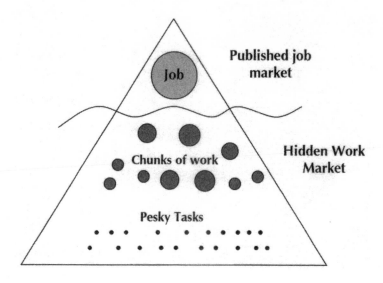

the tip of the iceberg just sticking out above it.

Small dots at the bottom of the triangle represent the organization's pesky little tasks which fall through the cracks because of time pressures or because they aren't part of anyone's job description. The fact that they don't get done is annoying, but it doesn't have a significant impact on the organization.

The circles in the middle represent small annoyances that have grown over time into real obstacles to productivity and efficiency. Although these "chunks of work" have not yet reached the point where something absolutely has to be done about them, they are causing problems.

Eventually the chunks in the middle grow until the adverse consequences of not doing something about them become apparent. Then they are bundled together to form a job which shows up in the published job market—*unless* the work is contracted out to a vendor or a consultant before it reaches that point.

The middle, where work is emerging, is the most fertile ground for new opportunities. It is the place where Ground of Your Own Choosing work-seekers focus their attention because it is there that they can connect directly with the people who understand the organization's needs and position themselves as a resource for fulfilling them. In the middle they aren't in competition with hundreds or thousands of others, as they would be if they confined themselves to looking only for the work that has coalesced into a job at the tip of the iceberg. The only obstacle they face is the organization's ability to pay for their services, and there are many possibilities for creating work within an organization's budget for those who are not locked into jobthink. A pilot project to begin establishing a relationship, taking on one or more bundles of work for a monthly fee, being contracted hourly on an as-needed basis, are just a few examples.

The following story shows how this can happen. A consultant spoke at the regional convention of a professional association, and afterward one of the managers in the audience came up to her and praised her presentation. The two of them exchanged business cards.

The next day the consultant sent a follow-up email thanking the manager and offering to meet with her to find out more about the needs of her organization. In the meeting that followed, they brainstormed ideas about areas where the consultant could contribute, i.e., chunks of work she could take on. In a number of subsequent conversations, the two of them considered various scenarios for working together, but budget constraints within the manager's organization prevented them from proceeding. Yet with each conversation, the relationship between the two of them deepened, and the desire to work together grew stronger. Then one day, quite unexpectedly, the consultant got a call from the manager asking her to do several components of an in-house training program she was directing.

The consultant succeeded by operating at the nexus where the needs of the organization and outside resources come together. If she had waited for an RFP (Request for Proposal, the consulting equivalent of a job posting) for the training program, she would have been in competition with others for the work. As it was, she was the very first person the manager thought of when the training budget was approved. Moreover, in the process of creating this opportunity, the consultant positioned herself as a resource for future projects and forged the kind of professional alliance that makes looking for work enjoyable rather than burdensome.

This kind of work-search begins with a spark between two individuals. It's followed by a meeting in which both parties sit on the same side of the table and look at a problem together. How different this is from the job interview where people with different agendas sit on opposite sides of a desk! The meeting provides an opportunity for each side to clarify their needs, consider options, and begin establishing a rapport which will lead to an ongoing dialogue. Once this is accomplished, opportunities naturally follow.

No Meeting, No Action

Basically jobthinkers have it backwards. They send out resumes, lots of them, to try to generate a single opposite-sides-of-the-table meeting, i.e., a job interview. What they need to be doing is what the consultant did—seize every opportunity to set up same-side-of-the-table meetings to create professional relationships which become potential sources of work.

One of the best tools for doing this is the information interview, a technique developed by Daniel Porot in his book, *The PIE Method*, and described in Richard Bolles' *What Color Is Your Parachute?* The information interview is a brief conversation for the *sole* purpose of finding out more from someone who is doing a kind of work that interests you or who belongs to an organization or field you would like to know more about. Although it is highly effective, the information interview is often misused as a ploy to make a sales pitch.

The following scenario is all too common. A person looking for a job aggressively networks to connect to someone he sees as a "hot prospect." He wants to score—big (think Megabucks). He requests an information interview with the person, but his real objective is to get face-to-face with this guy, the same way a car salesman tries to get a customer into the showroom. He wants to impress him with a stunning presentation of his abilities and get an offer. After schmoozing about sports, politics, mutual friends, etc. he goes into a spiel pitching his experience and then asks in a folksy, casual way if there's an opening for a guy like him. Long before he moves in for the kill, the person who is having this "information interview" inflicted upon him has already figured out he's been conned, and the moment he does, for all practical purposes the conversation is over. No meaningful dialogue has taken place, and no real connection will have been made when the jobseeker leaves. Instead the interviewee will be left thinking, "Why do I waste my time?"

Done correctly, the information interview is pure inquiry. It's an exercise in asking the right questions, the kind that tell you what you need to know to make good business decisions. The discipline being practiced is *research*, not sales, and when people trust that this is the motivation for meeting with them, they are much more likely to be engaged and helpful. Information interviewing provides knowledge which will prove invaluable in determining where you fit in the marketplace and how you can best present your qualifications. It is of great benefit in shaping, directing, and energizing any sort of work search, from free-agency to long-term employment (a.k.a. a job).

There are two kinds of questions in an information interview. The first is designed to help a person determine if the work he is investigating is right for him. Asking someone about himself and his organization, how he came to be where he is, what he likes and doesn't like about his role, etc. are examples of questions which can help to make choices such as:

- Do I want to consider this as a possibility?

- How much time and energy do I want to invest in it?

- Am I excited enough by what I have heard to maintain
  a dialogue with this person and talk to others in the field?

The second kind of question helps a person understand the nature of a specific opportunity so that he can decide if he wants to position himself as someone who is suited to apply for it. Questions about the sorts of education, training, and experience looked favorably upon by the organization, the problems and challenges encountered on a regular basis, the skills and attributes needed to overcome them, will help him be able to:

- Speak with clarity to the ways his background matches the work.

- Give specific examples of how he has used the skills the work requires.

- Use appropriate language and terminology.

Information interviews are easy to set up, cost nothing but the expense of traveling there and back, require a relatively small amount of time, and give in return a wealth of knowledge and renewed confidence.

A few years out of college, Jeremy got an entry-level marketing distribution position with a large corporation in the food industry. It turned out that the job entailed little more than stocking shelves in grocery stores with junk food, and over time, the work became onerous to him, especially after he started to practice a regimen of healthy eating.

Jeremy decided to use information interviewing to help him find a new direction. He started out by talking to the owners of the health food stores he frequented. These conversations taught him a lot about the health food and supplement industry and provided a list of companies he thought he might like to work for.

The store owners connected him with sales representatives working for these companies. Conversations with salespeople gave him a much clearer understanding of how the work compared and contrasted with his current job and confirmed his desire to make the change.

The sales representatives in turn directed him to their managers, and by the time Jeremy came to conducting information interviews with people who were in a position to hire him, he felt well-prepared. When several of them pointed out the importance of having a knowledge of herbs, he took courses in the subject and let them know he had met those requirements. A short time later he was offered a job with one of the companies.

He started out knowing almost nothing about the health food industry, aside from the fact that he liked it, and ended up being perceived as someone who really knew what he was talking about. He accomplished this transformation one conversation at a time, and he had control over the process every step of the way. He kept himself moving toward his goal by always setting up the next meeting. He didn't have to wait for a response. It was always in his power to initiate forward motion, and ultimately it was his own actions that attracted work to him. This was very different from the jobthinker who waits for someone to provide the next job, project, or assignment. Jeremy chose instead to operate from the ground of his own choosing. Like a true entrepreneur, he went out and made it happen.

CHAPTER IV

Throw Out Your Resume and Stop Networking

No employer wants to know what you have in common with everyone else. He or she wants to know what makes you unique and individual.
                    Richard Bolles
                    What Color Is Your Parachute?

Communities of practice are the next step, and they are different in significant ways (from networks). They are communities, which means that people make a commitment to be available to each other, to offer support, to share learning, to consciously develop new knowledge. They are there not only for their own needs, but for the needs of others.
                    Margaret J. Wheatley
                    Finding Our Way

The first thing you can do to root out jobthink is to eliminate the word "job" from your vocabulary. Why? Because the language we use shapes our thinking.

If you look up the word "job," you'll notice that many of its meanings—a task, something to be done, an assignment—apply to work both as it existed in the pre-Industrial Age and will exist in the future. Yet the word is still most often used in the sense that it took on during the Industrial Age—a permanent, full-time position with a single employer.

When I make the case against jobthink to student audiences, they get it right away and immediately begin spelling out j-o-b instead of saying the word. They understand that the world of work has changed, and they appreciate hearing someone tell the truth about it.

People in whom jobthink is more deeply entrenched, however, may have to practice the discipline of correcting themselves every time they say the word. Since the best way to get rid of a bad habit is to replace it with good one, it helps to swap the word "job" for the word "work." "Job" bears roughly the same relation to "work" as "orange" does to "fruit." If you go to the grocery store with your heart set on oranges and a bad winter has caused a shortage of them, you will end up disappointed. If you go looking for fruit instead, you are likely to find a variety of ways to satisfy your taste and appetite.

Thinking of your career as "work" opens up the possibility that it can be much more than a succession of boxes on an organizational chart. It means you won't necessarily pursue only one occupation, and you won't expect to stay in one place because you understand that the average working life today is longer than the life span of the average business (Drucker). It gives you the freedom, with all the burdens that come with it, to integrate your work and your life and better align who you are with what you do.

Throw Out Your Resume

The jobthinker directs all his attention at a single form of documentation, a resume. He overlooks alternative ways of communicating his value in his quest to make the resume as perfect as possible. This obsession is unfortunate not only because it means he is putting all his eggs in one rather fragile basket, but also because he is likely to lose sight of the "forest" (what he has to offer) for the "trees" (wording, layout, font, format, stock, etc.)

It is because people get hung up on seeing one or two 8^1/$_2$ x 11 sheets of paper as the golden key to a magic door that I told the group of Bentley College alumni (see Preface) that they would be better off throwing out their resumes. I of course didn't intend it to be taken literally. I understand that a resume is necessary for presenting your credentials to an organization where you would like to find work, *if*—and it's a big if—you are approaching it as an individual, i.e., on a person-to-business basis. What I meant was, don't let the resume control your thinking. File it under Business Forms, and the next time a friend or colleague offers to pass it along to someone, say to them, "What I'd really like is to have a brief conversation with the person instead." Then the resume would be something you would leave behind as a reminder of your qualifications *after* the meeting.

The resume should be considered merely a part of the etiquette of work search, something you have to have to follow the rules. When it is seen as the engine that drives it, when it starts to control the scope and direction of a career, something is seriously out of whack. Form and protocol have replaced innovation and initiative.

What would happen if you could rid yourself of the time-honored, sacred cow of job-search? What if you got off the post-and-wait merry-go-round? If you didn't rely on a resume, what would you do?

- You would have to take active control of your work-search.

- You would dig deeper into yourself to discover exactly what you want to do and why you are uniquely suited to do it.

- You would analyze your career history to bring out what is most valuable.

- Instead of listing skills and accomplishments on a piece of paper and expecting someone else to figure out how to make them fit, you would make those connections yourself.

- You would seek out new ways of presenting yourself in the market place. Virtual postings would be replaced by real meetings with live people!

- Rather than a chronology of what you what you did 5, 10, 15, or 20 years ago, you would develop a plan which would enable you talk to a prospective employer about what you can do right now and will do in the future.

- Your resume would be only a part of a comprehensive portfolio of self-marketing tools designed to gain and sustain interest: a concise statement of features and benefits, a professional bio, targeted promotional letters, testimonials, etc.

The resume belongs to the Industrial Age, when lifelong employment in clearly defined jobs was the norm. That age has passed, and exclusive reliance on it will only limit possibilities, not open doors. It has too narrow an application to be effective in today's highly competitive business environment.

There *is* value in a resume, but it's not what people think. The resume can be a useful tool for developing a strategy for how you are going to market yourself.

Imagine you've just walked into a hiring manager's office for an interview. You notice that your resume is sitting on his desk, and you smile and say to yourself, "All the effort I put into getting my resume just right has paid off." Once you are seated, however, the manager picks up the document you worked so hard on and rips it in half. "I'm not interested in what you did in the past," he says. "I want to know what you can do for me now."

Can you answer that question? You can if you've used the resume for the right purpose, as a means for learning how to articulate and substantiate your selling points. The real value of a resume is to *you*, not to a prospective employer. Putting one together is an exercise in taking ownership of your expertise so that you can market it effectively to someone else. It is not an employer's responsibility to connect the dots of your qualifications and experience and figure out how they fit. It's yours.

Stop Networking

Networking is not nearly as effective as the experts who continually hype its value claim. What they are touting as a panacea is actually a myth. The networking approach being sold these days is not only dull and unimaginative, but also outdated. It does not take into consideration the changing realities in the world of work.

The term, "networking," has been around for so long that we've ceased to think about what it really means, and, more importantly, to ask ourselves if it's something we want to subject ourselves to. The word suggests casting a net over people who we think will be a "good catch" and hauling them in. It's no wonder that when people are asked for adjectives they associate with networking, they come up with words like "self-serving," "mercenary," and "hard-edged." There are five good reasons to stop networking.

Reason One

It doesn't work nearly as well as it used to. The problem that fishermen face today offers an appropriate analogy. Fishing has always been a difficult business to be in, but nowadays, with declining stocks, it's harder than ever. A point of diminishing returns has been reached in many parts of the world as more fisherman are chasing fewer fish. In the same way, with each new round of layoffs, the number of people who are out there "fishing" for contacts grows while the "stocks" of people available to respond to them dwindles. When jobs were plentiful, networking had a much better chance of success than it does now. The workplace is simply no longer the productive "fishing ground" it used to be.

Reason Two

Because networking narrows its sights on getting connected with the person who can steer you to the perfect job or the lucrative account, the energy that is single-mindedly devoted to zeroing in on Mr. or Ms. Right results in a kind of tunnel-vision which prevents you from seeing the entire panorama of possibilities. Jobs as we have known them are being replaced by a multitude of choices, e.g., freelancing, contract employment, consulting, etc. As this trend continues, the line between the work-seeker and the entrepreneur will become less sharply defined, and individuals looking for work will need to think of themselves as independent business entities whether they are self-employed or not. Work-seekers, whether formally or functionally in business for themselves, will have to cultivate as many resources as possible to support their objectives because the only real work security will be in having a safety net of strong professional relationships.

Reason Three

Networking is fundamentally self-serving. The person who is out there networking has the attitude, "I'm talking to you because I think you might be able to do something for me." Networking is not about a reciprocal exchange that promises lasting benefits to both parties. Like so much of the thinking that goes on in the business world, it's short-term. The question it seeks to answer is, "How can this person help me to get what I want?" instead of, "Is this a person I would like to learn from and teach so that both our professional lives will be enriched as a result?"

Reason Four

Networking requires making value judgments based on inadequate information. Imagine you're at a networking function, and there are a lot of people there. Time is limited, so you have to choose who to focus your energy on and who to disregard. To make the decision, however, all you really have to go on is what's printed on a name tag. How can you begin to know whether a person might be able to add value to your professional life based on such scanty evidence?

Years ago I regularly attended a networking group where managers who were either out of work or facing imminent unemployment spent their Saturday mornings standing around shoulder to shoulder with hundreds of others in the same predicament. Because I was in private practice and not connected with a big name corporation, many of them pointedly ignored me. From the information on my name tag there was no way they could know that, as a career counselor, I had extensive contacts, some of them with people they wanted to talk to. Later, when I was asked to address this same group on the subject of networking, I called their attention to the problem of making judgments about people based on the information on a name tag. I went on to enumerate some of my many connections, and I suddenly became much more popular!

Reason Five

Most people aren't very good at networking. It feels awkward to them, and when people aren't comfortable with a behavior they may do it for a short time, but they rarely keep it up, and no activity can produce lasting benefits unless it is pursued consistently. In the twenty-five years I've been in practice, I've seen a lot more guilt about networking, i.e., "I really should be doing more of it," than sustained action.

It's not just introverts who have problems reaping benefits from networking. Both extroverts and introverts suffer from blind spots. The talent for working a room, admired by those who don't have it, is often not productive. The people who flutter from person to person as effortlessly as a butterfly usually have trouble remembering what was said in the exchanges, and they are rarely good about following up with the contacts they make. Attentive listeners, on the other hand, are generally good at follow-up but struggle with starting conversations and go mute when the time comes to speak about themselves.

For some people, networking generates so much anxiety it becomes counter-productive. It undermines self-confidence and, when you're nervous in a situation, it shows. It's better to make a coffee date with someone whose company you enjoy and whose professional abilities you respect than it is to force yourself to attend a meeting where you feel ill at ease.

Community-Building: A Better Way

Networking is like a ladder. You set out to climb from rung to rung, ever higher, until you reach your goal.

Community-building is like a round table. You invite people into your circle based on shared interests and values.

Networking at best is sociability with a purpose. Everybody has had the experience of trying to have a conversation with someone who is looking over your shoulder to see if there's someone else in the room he'd rather be talking to. That's what networking is like. If you're networking, you're always on the lookout for opportunities.

In community-building, you and the other person are present to each other, and the exchange is mutually beneficial. Opportunities come to you because you have surrounded yourself with people who have a genuine connection to your values, interests, and life's mission.

Community-building is about putting together a circle of nurturing affiliations. For it to flourish there must be absolutely no sense of urgency. The relationship must be based on a gut-level attraction to another person. It can't be forced, and it has no timeline. It grows at its own pace.

For the community-builder, every encounter has potential. Trade shows, conventions, banquets are good places for community-building, but so are soccer games, school plays, and chance encounters in the grocery store. You're just as likely to find someone to add to your circle sitting next to you on the plane on the way to a conference as you are at the event itself.

Community-building begins when you are drawn to a person for no other reason than you like what they have to say or how they handle themselves. There must always be a sincere connection between you and the other person, even if initially you are not able to identify

Networking	Community-Building
Hierarchical (ladder)	Collegial (round table or concentric circles)
Value of the connection based on how well-placed the contact is perceived to be	Value of the connection based on shared interests and concerns
Self-serving	Mutually beneficial
Narrowly targeted	Open to possibilities
Depends on promotion	Depends on attraction
Artificial	Genuine
Short-term	Long-term

exactly what it is. The important thing is that you honor the fact that there is something there that attracts you, and that you follow up on it by calling, sending a note, making a lunch date, etc.

When Elizabeth was starting to build her marketing practice, she found her graphic artist over a bowl of potato salad at a picnic when, spoon in hand, the person next to her in the buffet line mentioned that she was a watercolorist and was taking a course in Adobe Photoshop®. It was the beginning of what turned out to be a long and productive relationship, but it didn't happen right away. As she was cultivating it, Elizabeth found it helpful to ask herself three questions:

1. *Would I like having this person enter the circle of my community for the next five minutes?* Elizabeth had already said yes to that question before she got to the end of the buffet line.

2. *Is this someone I'd enjoy having enter the circle of my community again?* The yes to this question came the week after the party when Elizabeth found the artist's business card in her purse and called her to see if she'd like to get together.

3. *Is this someone I'd like to have enter the circle of my community on a regular basis?* The yes to this question came after several meetings during which the two of them talked about everything under the sun, including how neither of them really knew that much about what they were doing, which seemed like a good basis on which to start working together. It wasn't long after that Elizabeth realized that this chance meeting had led her to the ideal resource to design a logo for one of her clients.

Notice that throughout the process, Elizabeth's focus remained squarely on building the relationship, and she never went further than the next step.

For genuine community-building to happen there must be no agenda. Regardless of the conversation, an agenda makes the exchange less genuine. The moment you make the decision to go to a meeting or social event for the purpose of drumming up business, you've stacked the deck against making the kind of spontaneous, sincere connection which will be of the greatest benefit to you over time. Having an agenda forces you to expend your energy trying to sniff out the decision-makers in the crowd and makes you less receptive to meeting that person you are naturally attracted to because you both speak the same language. It interferes with your instincts which will serve you better in the long run. If you're not enjoying yourself at an event, you're probably networking. Networking is

THROW OUT YOUR RESUME AND STOP NETWORKING

draining. Community-building is energizing.

Nine Actions That Support Community-Building

1. Approach every encounter with an open mind, understanding that each one offers the possibility for community-building.

2. Pay attention when someone says or does something that resonates with you, and write down what it was that got your attention.

3. At every gathering or event, try to identify three people you feel comfortable approaching with the goal of simply having a pleasant conversation.

4. Replace professional or social activities where you feel ill at ease with ways of interacting that are more comfortable.

5. After every business gathering, set yourself the goal of following up within a week to ten days with at least one person you have identified as someone you might like to add to your community. Make it a priority.

6. Keep the focus on the next step in building the relationship, and remember that the purpose of the exchange is simply to learn more about each other and find ways of being helpful.

7. Make sure that the person you are thinking of adding to your circle is someone you really want a relationship with by continually doing reality checks on the genuineness of the connection.

8. Record highlights of your meetings and write down things you'd like to talk about with the person based on your growing understanding of the ways that your interests intersect.

9. If you have made several attempts to add someone to your circle, and you don't feel that your interest is reciprocated, execute some form of closure.

A Community-Building Story

Whenever I come across an article that speaks directly to my core beliefs, it's an exciting event for me, and I often want to share my thoughts with the writer. Now that many publications provide the email addresses of authors, it's easy to do.

When I emailed the author of an article in the business section of a major newspaper that got my attention, she wrote back to thank me and mentioned that she happened to live not far from me. Based solely on the fact that I liked the way she thought, I suggested we get together. I got no response.

A few months later, I read another article that rang my chimes, and it came as no surprise that it was by the same person. What particularly interested me in the second article was her story about how a casual encounter with the CEO of a multimillion dollar company in Staples® that started out with a conversation over what brand of CD's to buy resulted in a mutually beneficial exchange. I wrote her again, explaining that I was working on a new approach to networking, and I told her I would really appreciate her thoughts on the subject. She responded immediately and apologized for not picking up on my first invitation to get together.

We met for lunch and I was so busy enjoying her brilliant mind that my plan to talk to her about my ideas went out the window. As we were saying our goodbyes in the parking lot, she again apologized for not responding to my first invitation and explained that every time she publishes an article she gets more than a thousand emails in response, virtually all of them wanting something from her. In the case of the one where she described her encounter with the CEO in Staples®, they wanted to know what the two of them talked about, they wanted her to provide them with a referral to him, they even wanted to know which Staples the meeting had occurred at, as if by going there the same thing might happen to them! These people were networking just the way they had been taught.

What they failed to understand was how they invaded her privacy and exhausted and even appalled her.

As I drove away I realized I had been given exactly what I needed to make the case for replacing networking with community-building. Over a thousand people tried to network their way to this woman in hopes of getting something from her, and they got nowhere. I approached her from the mindset of community-building, wanting nothing more than to exchange ideas, and I had lunch with her.

CHAPTER V

Beyond Jobthink

*Security no longer resides in the job (any job). It resides
in your ability to add value to what some organization
does . . . . The skills you need to develop for this value-
adding task aren't the old job-based skills . . . . They are
actually skills that are less often associated with being
a good employee than they are with being a successful
small-business operator.*

William Bridges
Creating You & Co.

A trip becomes a journey after you've lost your luggage.
Anonymous
quoted by William Bridges

I've just lost my job as a middle-level manager with a company
I've been with for eighteen years. They closed our local opera-
tions and moved what we did offshore . . . . What am I to do?"
Thus writes a middle-aged man to Carl Schramm, President of the
Kauffman Foundation, a non-profit organization dedicated to foster-
ing entrepreneurship.

Schramm shares his response in his book, *The Entrepreneurial Imperative: How America's Economic Miracle Will Reshape the World
(and Change Your Life)*: "The single most important piece of advice
I can offer you is—you should approach this next stage of your working life as if you were an entrepreneurial company in startup mode.
You need to plan how to enter the market and make sure your value

is seen by your customer (your new employer), recognizing that the new employer could very well be you." Schramm encourages him not to look back "with nostalgia" on a time that has past, but to put his energy into "re-inventing himself" by acquiring new skills and knowledge and a new understanding of "his relationship to the labor market."

His message is clear—*become an entrepreneur!*

This rallying cry is also taken up by Jeff Taylor, the founder of the job-search website, Monster.com. On the opening page of his book, *Monster Careers: How to Land the Job of Your Life*, just inside the front cover in crisp, bold statements, he lists the cornerstones of the new outlook for achieving work security in today's "post long-term job" era: "Think like a Free Agent," "Train like an Athlete," "Prepare like a Marketer," and "Work like an Entrepreneur."

Schramm, Taylor, and others are echoing what I have been saying up to this point—stop thinking in terms of a job, and begin to think of work in an entirely different way.

What they are *not* saying is that this is a huge undertaking which involves dealing with some very uncomfortable feelings. There's nothing in either Schramm or Taylor about the transformation that has to take place inside a person before entrepreneurial thinking has a chance of taking root. They go no further than identifying a set of tasks. Their advice is all about how to respond to external change in external ways, and it ends up being plodding and formulaic like what you find in traditional job-search manuals. The truth is, there's no going from jobthinker to entrepreneur in ten easy steps. It can't be done by the numbers.

No one seriously believes that the recipient of Schramm's advice is going to hit himself on the forehead and say, "Eureka, that's it! Why didn't *I* think of it! I'll become an entrepreneur!" Even if he accepts the idea that he can't go back to what he did before, he will experience an indeterminate period of grief, fear, and confusion as he struggles to come to terms with the demise of his work life as he has known it. No wonder no one wants to talk about it! We like business problems to have sharply defined solutions that can be neatly summed up in bullet points.

Taylor of Monster.com encapsulates the new paradigm of work in a collection of slogans and gives us a handy-dandy acronym, FAME, standing for *F*ree-agent, *A*thlete, *M*arketer, and *E*ntrepreneur, just in case we forget. He treats these ideas like the motivational mantras on the "success art" posters you see for sale in the mall that show snow-covered mountains mirrored in a tranquil lake with an eagle soaring in the foreground and the word, "Leadership," in bold block letters across the bottom, or a rowing crew on a golden, glowing river at sunset with the caption, "Teamwork." As anyone who's ever been a leader or functioned as a member of a team knows, saying the word and doing the deed are two very different things. People who have been hit by the workquake need more than a pretty picture on the wall.

Take John, for example, a laid-off computer programmer who was the subject of a recent article in the business section of a local newspaper. He has been looking for work for two years. How would these slogans apply to him?

Think like a free agent.
Since losing his job, John has sent out an average of four resumes a week. In the same period he has had only half a dozen interviews and received just one offer, a low-paying temporary job.

Is John thinking like a free agent? Hardly. His entire focus is on getting the same kind of job he had before. He's trying to recreate the past, to get his old life back, because it's all he knows. Unfortunately, the work he did was highly specialized and is now obsolete, and the fact that while he was employed he didn't keep up with new technologies means that his work life as he knew it was over the moment he was let go.

For John, the real work of "thinking like a free agent" can't begin until he recognizes that the door to the past is closed, locked, and barred. Only after he has dealt with this on an emotional level will he be able to see the doors which could open to him in the future.

Train like an athlete.

At first glance, John's commitment to sending out resumes week in and week out may seem like a pretty good career "fitness program." In fact, he credits the longevity of his job-search to being able to stick with a daily routine of research and resume-tweaking.

Two years of tweaking a resume??!!

If you're an athlete, you don't get stronger by doing the same exercises day after day. You do it by steadily upping the level of difficulty. John has kept himself at the same place for two years, and he expects to get stronger? It won't happen.

It's true that by chasing published job openings, John is getting a certain amount of mild "aerobic exercise," but he's not building strength in the marketplace by enhancing his skills, nor is he improving flexibility by going beyond traditional job-search.

John will begin to "train like an athlete" only after he sees that what he has been doing up to this point is the equivalent of running in place. Then he can start looking for ways, little ones at first, to increase the distance.

Prepare like a marketer.

In sending out all those resumes, John has produced an exhaustive (and no doubt exhaust*ing*) direct mail campaign, but his rate of response has been well below the threshold that would justify the cost of postage, much less the time and energy he's expending.

Marketers talk about the Four P's—product, price, promotion, and pipelines (distribution)—and for John to begin "preparing like a marketer" he will have to put them in order. He will have to figure out where his *product*—himself—fits in the marketplace. He will have to know its *value* and how to communicate it to others. He will have to explore different ways of *making it visible*. Finally, he will have to open up more than one *channel of distribution* by considering kinds of work that are different from what he was doing before he got laid off. But before he can do this, he will have to be open to using this period of his life to reinvent himself.

John is not sure whether he wants to further his education, but he has decided at least to entertain the idea. He is thinking about taking a week off from his research-and-resume drudgery to look at college offerings and do some soul-searching. It's a good first step.

Work like an entrepreneur.
One positive move John has made is to use the time on his hands to volunteer for a local watchdog group. This has given him the opportunity to learn more about non-profit organizations. Unfortunately, whenever he talks about his volunteer work, he describes himself sardonically as "the world's oldest intern," which indicates that he does not see the possibility that it could be a stepping-stone to something else. Just as he has drawn a line limiting the scope of his work-search, he has circumscribed his volunteer role. His interest in non-profits, if cultivated, could offer opportunities to expand not only his employment options, but also his level of satisfaction in the work he does. But his thinking has stopped right at the point where entrepreneurial action should begin. John will start to "work like an entrepreneur" when he asks himself, "Where could this lead? How could I develop this opportunity? What leverage could this give me in other markets?"

Being In Transition

If asked, John would say that he is "in transition," but he would be using the term strictly as a euphemism for being out of work. He has not really entered into transition. Authentic transition begins with an ending, in this case the end of jobthink, and this is something he has not done. By denying that the workquake has brought an end to the professional life he was accustomed to and attempting to avoid the period which follows in which he is suspended between what was and what will be, he cuts himself off from the creative space that makes reinventing himself possible.

Becoming an entrepreneur is not a decision, but a journey. It cannot be done with the flip of a switch. Before he can see himself as transmutable, John will have to weather a lot of internal resistance to get to a place of acceptance within himself. To get through this often dark and sometimes exciting period, it would help him to understand what successful transition looks and feels like so that he can know how to sustain himself while he is going through it and stay in it long enough to emerge with something truly new.

Being in transition lies at the heart of every career process, whether it's looking for work, starting a business, or adjusting the demands of work to fit changes in lifestyle. Few people, however, understand what transition is really about. Most confuse it with change.

Change occurs at a specific time and place in the external world and is over relatively quickly. *Transition* is the internal process of coming to grips with change. It has no timetable.

Change is what happens when your boss calls you into his office at 4 PM on Friday to tell you that your job has been eliminated. *Transition* is what you experience on Monday morning, and an indeterminate number of days, weeks, and months thereafter, as you roam around the house not knowing what to do with yourself. It is, in the words of William Bridges, a "psychological reorientation to change." You are in transition, not because you are out of work, but because of what's going on inside you—anger, fear, relief, excitement, confusion, disbelief—as you try to adapt to change. Whether or not you are able to do this consciously and intentionally is another matter.

To be truly in transition means two things. First, it means accepting the loss of identity, influence, power, position, income, routine, and sense of worth that comes with having your work life as you have known it *end*. It also means allowing yourself to feel the feelings associated with that loss.

Second, it means recognizing at the same time that stepping forward boldly into the messy process of transition is a prelude to taking charge of your professional life so that you can become more of who you want to be.

Transition Begins With An Ending

One of the reasons people don't do transition well is that they don't do endings. There are many aspects to a successful transition, but the most important is that first something has to end. Without an ending, there is no transition, and when there is no transition, *something has changed, but nothing is different*. To move forward, we must fully participate in the death of some entrenched attitude, belief, or way of being in the world.

One morning I was scheduled to make a presentation at a local bank, and I was running late. The traffic was very heavy on the main road, but I knew I would be turning off onto Bearse's Way before I hit the worst of it. A mile or so before I reached the intersection, there was a digital sign as big as the side of a house with the words, "Bearse's Way Closed Seek Alternate Route." I saw the sign—I couldn't have missed it if I tried—but I decided it didn't apply to me.

The road leading to the bank turned off only a short distance down Bearse's Way. Surely I could get that far. They wouldn't close the road to "important" people like me. There had to be some way around the highway department's no. I was determined to do it my way, until I saw that the pavement on Bearse's Way was torn up, and a barricade had been put there to keep cars from entering.

I suddenly found that I couldn't think of any other way to get where I was going!

Would the next side street connect through? Could I get there by cutting through the mall parking lot? What if the old story about the tourist asking directions from the native of Maine were true, and I actually couldn't get there from here?

I felt lost and confused, just the way people feel when they come to an intersection in their professional lives and find a familiar path blocked. In my moment of blankness, I experienced a tiny bit of the what-on-earth-will-I-do-now feeling they live with every day. Intellectually I knew there had to be some way of getting where I needed to go, but that wasn't how it *felt*, and my feelings had been in the driver's seat from the moment I read the sign and decided to ignore it!

My refusal to face reality that morning helped me to understand why people will watch their company's revenues fall off, their colleagues being let go, etc. and stay on, even though the work has stopped being rewarding, or try to "sneak through" until the kids finish college or to retirement. Before we can seek an alternate route, we first have to see with our own eyes that the way is closed. It doesn't matter if a spouse or a counselor or a co-worker sees it. We have to see it for ourselves because we are the ones who have to be willing to live with the deer-in-the-headlights feeling until it passes. Only then will we be able to fully engage our heads, our talents, our experience, and our resources in finding a new direction.

Gerald owned a printing business in a small town for thirty years. He had a loyal clientele and an excellent reputation, but changes in technology were causing his business to dry up. He tried to ignore or rationalize the signs, but it wasn't working, and he was unable to think of any other recourse. When he finally accepted that his business would never be the way it was before, he was able to see that his longstanding involvement in the community, an important part of his earlier success, had provided him with a wealth of contacts, and that tapping into them could offer a number of "alternate routes" he hadn't thought of. The grip of panic loosened, and he began to talk about his situation in positive terms and take concrete steps toward the future.

Changes in the world of work are resulting in closed roads for a lot of people. How can they provide alternate routes for themselves? If I'd been driving a more expensive car the morning I was trying to get to the bank I might have had a GPS to guide me. What would it be like if you created a "CPS" (Career Positioning System) for yourself to help you get your bearings professionally?

- You would make experimentation a regular part of your professional life. Anything you do to experiment is good practice—even something as simple as doing a routine task in a new way or including people you would not normally include in a meeting. Experimentation feeds your creativity and keeps you limber for those times when something comes along that requires you to stretch yourself.

- You would venture off the beaten path more often. This would give you a better understanding of the territory and confidence in your ability to find your way around. Consequently you wouldn't be so afraid of getting lost.

- You would stop to ask for directions. Finding yourself at an impasse, you would get help instead of stubbornly trying random paths that could actually take you farther away from where you need to be.

- You would learn about how you fit in the big picture of the organization you work for by having conversations with people outside your immediate sphere to identify other areas where your abilities could be valuable.

- You would "diversify" your "career portfolio" by conscientiously working toward improving your skills through self-study and formal education.

- You would conduct your own performance audits periodically, asking yourself where and how you make the greatest contribution.

Ending Jobthink

In *Transitions: Making Sense of Life's Changes*, William Bridges writes, "We take [endings] too seriously by confusing them with finality, when actually they are, or at least have the potential to be, the starting point for a journey of growth and renewal. New growth cannot take root on ground still covered with old habits, attitudes and outlooks, [and] endings are the clearing process."

Bridges' investigation of transition came about as a result of his own ending, his decision to leave his career as a college professor. Finding himself, in the words of poet Matthew Arnold, "Wandering between two worlds, one dead,/The other powerless to be born" ("Stanzas From the Grande Chartreuse"), he set out to discover meaning in this experience, and in doing so provided a model for those who are caught between the death of jobs in the Industrial Age and their rebirth as work in the Information Age.

Transition offers no instant answers or short cuts, nor does it ignore the struggle that accompanies rebirth. Instead it gives permission to feel a full range of feelings, from panic ("What if I never find work again?"), to exhilaration ("What if I could do something I really loved?"). It promotes the exploration of new possibilities without worrying about where it will lead. It encourages us to learn about ourselves and begin to fill in the blank canvas of an in-between space in our lives.

Before we can come up with innovative ways to get across the chasm created by the workquake to more secure ground, we must first end jobthink, the number one obstacle to reinventing ourselves. Its persistence is the primary reason people are ineffective in finding work. "Nothing happens without an ending," Bridges tells us, and what needs to end is looking at our professional life as a series of jobs. The jobthinker who continues on the well-worn path of traditional job-search will keep spinning his wheels in the mud of employment practices, and even if he does find another job he will remain vulnerable.

But it will not be enough just to stop thinking in terms of a job. We must be vigilant about not chasing *anything* that makes us dependent on something outside ourselves for our security. Suppose a jobthinker heeds the call to become an entrepreneur. Suppose he becomes a consultant and lands a big account and begins looking to that one relationship for security. He's right back where he started. There has been no real transition because there has not been an ending in the way he *thinks* about work. He has simply circled back. He has a new address, but it's the same house of cards.

Only when we come to rely on our own capacity to generate the work we get paid to do will the transformation from jobthinker to entrepreneur be complete. Being an entrepreneur means being innovative and accepting uncertainty, and embracing transition provides an opportunity to practice these behaviors. We begin to recreate our professional lives when we consciously choose to pass through the door marked "The End of Jobthink" into transition.

Creative Space

When I talk about the uncharted territory that follows an ending, I like to borrow an idea from William Bridges and use *The Wizard of Oz* as an allegory of transition. I start by asking people to remember what happens in the movie after Dorothy has been taken up into the funnel cloud of the tornado and dropped into Oz with a sudden jolt. She steps out of the house and looks around at this strange and beautiful new land, and the first thing she says is, "Toto, I've a feeling we're not in Kansas any more." One of the ways you know you've entered the creative space of transition is that you can only describe where you are by saying where you are *not*.

Up to this point, the movie has been in black-and-white, and Dorothy's life has been depicted as drab and unfulfilled, but now she is in a world of dazzling Technicolor® where both exciting and frightening things happen. She sets off down the Yellow Brick Road in search of the Wizard, the "expert" who can tell her how to get back home, but in the end she learns, not from him, but from Glinda, the Good Witch of the North, that she can only get there by taking charge of her own destiny. She experiences many things in Oz, some pleasant, some not, yet it is through *all of them* that her life is transformed. Oz is the creative space of her transition from the old to the new.

We have a choice how to respond when we are faced with one of those I'm-not-in-Kansas-any-more situations. We can turn away, or we can look at it as creative space, the same way a painter looks at a blank canvas, a poet an empty page, or a musician a piano keyboard, i.e., as an invitation to draw, write, or compose.

We live in a culture that does not encourage us to consider a period of confusion and uncertainty as an impetus for inspiration. It conditions us rather to think of it as an impediment to moving forward on the track we've set for ourselves. There are many who miss out on the gratification the creative space has to offer because they set out to avoid it, or they are unable to stay with it, or they get lost in it and spiral down into depression and immobility.

Some try to force a solution. Their goal is to move as seamlessly as possible from an ending to a destination. They don't want to deal with the feelings that come with not knowing where they are or where they are headed. They're interested in the quickest way back to Kansas, not the wonders of Oz. Unfortunately, what these people usually create for themselves is not a transformed professional life but a rehash of the past.

Martha is a regional sales manager who routinely over-delivers and does not set limits around the hours she works. She was approaching burnout, and she pursued and landed a position she hoped would be less demanding with a different company. Six months later, however, she found herself in the same predicament, once again overwhelmed by work and without a life. Her choice to leave the first company was an ending of sorts, but she wound up recreating her old job in the new company because she did not take the time to understand that her problem has nothing to do with who she works for and everything to do with her. Until she uses the creative space of transition to explore *why* she finds it so difficult to achieve balance in her work life, nothing will change.

Others find it too difficult to remain in uneasiness and disorder, so they give up hope and make a conscious choice to turn back. The going gets tough, and they think, "I know I wasn't happy doing X, and I'd really like to see if I could do Y, but then again, maybe X wasn't so bad after all, and besides, if I try to do Y, I might have to take a cut in pay, go back to school, feel less competent, etc."

Alan, an unemployed senior manager, has spent much of his professional life on the road. He would like to have more time with his family, plus he is experiencing some health problems and needs to take better care of himself. He has made some progress in putting together a work life that will accomplish these goals, but the results have been mixed. Then one day a headhunter calls with an opportunity that comes with a big salary and a prestigious title, and he jumps at it. The temptation to circle back to the familiar, even though it's not what he really wants, is too strong.

Finally, there are those who are unable to cope with the loss of identity that comes with an ending. They feel groundless, and for them the experience is more like a void than a blank canvas. They don't ask for help and get stuck, unable to go either backwards or forwards.

Marvin is a former department manager who throughout his career has defined who he was by his work. He was offered an attractive buyout package in his mid-fifties and took it, even though he had no plan for what he was going to do in retirement. He thought that puttering, gardening, and golf would be enough, but he has found that time hangs heavy on his hands. Most of his friends have been connected with his work in some way, and since his retirement he has become increasingly isolated. Occasionally he gets together with his buddies from work, but it's not the same. His depression is becoming more severe, and he is growing irritable, drinking too much, spending a lot of time in front of the television.

These stories are examples of "paint-by-numbers" solutions to the blank canvas of the creative space. They attempt to stay within the lines of left-brain, linear thinking. They are not wrong, but they are incomplete because they do not contain the key elements of true creativity—light and air, space and time, perplexity and pondering. A more whole-brained approach, one that looks at the formlessness that follows an ending as an opportunity for creativity, is needed if a person is going to stay the course and bring forth something of lasting value.

Staying the Course

Artists have to learn to live with discomfort. They must embrace rather than avoid the uncertainty of not knowing how to begin or where they will end up. While they wait for clarity, they wonder, imagine, play with ideas, at the same time that they practice the discipline of their art. They stay with it until all the pieces come together as a finished work.

If you are going to reach the Ground of Your Own Choosing, you will need to be able to remain in the uncomfortable state of not-knowing until a clear picture begins to emerge. Like the artist, you will have to accept this as part of the process and keep in the forefront of your mind the rewards for persevering—a higher purpose, better alignment of who you are with what you do, a more balanced life, and professional security. One way to make these rewards more palpable to you is by drawing a picture or making a collage of images that represent how you want your professional life to look.

When Carlos, a senior executive, did this exercise he discovered that, although his life was packed solid with business and personal commitments, the picture he drew of what he wanted it to be was not crowded at all, and the things which were important to him stood out in sharp relief against an empty background. Although he had

85

been talking about slowing the pace for a long time, the spaciousness in his picture made the goal more concrete.

When Barbara, an event planner, made a collage representing her ideal professional life, it was anything but sparse. The page was filled with images of gardening, entertaining, art, etc., things which she has felt compelled to relinquish under the demands of her work. Like Carlos, the picture of her ideal was the opposite from the way her life really was.

Sarah, a laboratory manager, created her visual using PowerPoint®. On one slide, to symbolize her desire for doing work more directly connected to helping others, she used the image of an elderly woman with a cat in her lap because it reminded her of the time when she was an advocate for her grandmother in a nursing home.

An artist's vision takes shape through both trial and error and craft—a wild brush stroke or an unexpected blotch of color comes together with a carefully rendered drawing in a way that is unexpected. Likewise, the insights gained from pictures of an ideal professional life are realized in much the same way, through experimentation and discipline.

Experimentation is a safe way to try something new. All you have to do is take a few steps down the road to see how you like the view. It allows you to honor an inner nudge without bringing along the baggage of a commitment or feeling like you have to do it perfectly. You don't have to color inside the lines, you just have to color!

When Jeff's company told him the office where he worked would be closing in a year, he honored his desire to have more time to spend with his young children by looking for work that would be more flexible. He explored what people with skills like his were doing, and when he came across the website for a technical consultant, he was excited by the idea of being on his own. He started going to meetings of a local technology council where he could talk to people who were doing consulting work, and then he heard about a small business which was expanding and needed help setting up its network.

He'd often done this kind of thing for friends as a favor, but looking at it as a business opportunity was a new experience. He decided this would be a great way to take a small step toward independence, and he sought help in putting together a project proposal.

Experiments evolve. One thing leads to another. Jeff didn't make a master list of things to be done and check them off one at a time. He started by poking around on the Internet, and he only went as far as he could see. Each new activity flowed naturally from the last. He simply asked himself, "Am I sufficiently interested in this to take the next step? Where on the scale between frigid and boiling does this fall? Is it hot?" The momentum for doing the next thing depended on his level of engagement with the last.

As with every creative endeavor, there must be an underlying discipline which keeps experimentation constructive and prevents it from devolving into pointless dabbling. The artist constantly works at improving his technique, studies from the masters, gets feedback from peers, etc. He may not have a deadline, but he does have a goal, and he holds himself accountable for achieving it. This discipline, rather than constraining him, actually helps him to go with the flow and not push the river by forcing a particular outcome. He understands the wisdom of the old Chinese proverb, "Let the work teach you how to do it."

People who are successful in recreating themselves conscientiously participate in, rather than avoid, the creative space that follows an ending. They do this by learning more about themselves and expanding and deepening their professional relationships. These underpinnings enable them to stay in the creative space long enough to allow the next phase of their life to unfold.

After twenty-five years working for a large corporation, Jeanette began thinking it was time for her to find out what she really wanted to be "when she grew up." She had never much liked the corporate world, and when she made a list of priorities, the work she was doing wasn't high on it.

She learned about the creative space at a career transition workshop she attended with several friends who were also experiencing significant changes in their lives. What she took away from the day was an understanding of the importance of not rushing through the "gray, in-between, chaotic period" to get to the other side.

She is now pursuing things that interest her—creative writing, computer graphics, film, theater. For the moment, she wants to spend time just doing rather than thinking about what she should be doing. Although she does not yet know how all these interests will come together, she feels confident she's doing the right things and making progress. In the meantime, she's not in a hurry. She's having too much fun.

The creative space cannot be orchestrated and the methods for best utilizing it cannot be listed in a how-to manual. We can, however, learn to balance the openness of experimentation and the regimentation of discipline. To do this we embrace the creative tension of tacking back and forth between waiting for inspiration and driving ourselves to take the next step. Only in this way can we produce a unified whole, a finished picture which will give us great satisfaction.

CHAPTER VI

Authenticity

To become leaders of our own work lives, each of us needs to develop our capacity for authenticity. Awareness and authenticity allow us to translate our intentions into congruent behaviors and committed action.

Ken Cloke and Joan Goldsmith
The Art of Waking People Up

You have reached the Ground of Your Own Choosing the moment you know deep inside yourself, "I am the person to do this work." The path to this discovery runs through the fertile land of the creative space of transition, and if you follow it you will emerge with a better alignment between who you are and what you do.

The need for this alignment is a new phenomenon in human history. Prior to the early years of the last century, there was no need to know yourself well enough to be able to discern the kind of work you were well-suited for. If your father was a machinist or a tailor, you were one too. If you were a woman, you probably didn't work outside the home at all, unless it was necessary for survival.

As Peter Drucker has observed, the fact that we can now choose our vocation is an "unprecedented change in the human condition," one which future historians will view as even more significant than technology in shaping the era we live in. "For the first time, a substantial and rapidly growing number of people have choices. For the first time, they will have to manage themselves, and they are totally unprepared for it." (speech to the Leadership and Management Conference, 1999).

For a small percentage of the population, the alignment between self and work comes early in life and with an ease that is enviable. These are the people who have always known they wanted to be a nurse or an engineer or a pilot or a writer. Theirs is the straight career path that others envy.

Most of us, however, have to make do without this certainty. We reach adulthood, some of us even middle age, without knowing exactly what it is we want to be when we grow up. We latch on to something because it's handy or because it meets an immediate need and years later end up longing to do something other than what we fell into. The claims adjustor who went into the insurance business only because his brother-in-law offered him a job when he graduated from college, the contractor who joined the family business because his wife was pregnant, the elementary school teacher who chose education because she wanted to be able to work outside the home and raise a family, are just a few of many examples.

We may feel as if the whiz kids who experienced an early and definitive calling have wrecked the curve, forcing the rest of us to settle for a less than passing grade because we haven't been able to measure up to the standard they set. Yet the idea that they are the only ones who are destined to enjoy contentment in their work leads to misconceptions which can sabotage our efforts to claim our authenticity. If we believe that clarity comes only as a result of some kind of breakthrough, "aha" moment, we will overlook opportunities to learn and grow from our wanderings until we can at last position ourselves as *the* person to do a particular type of work.

A calling discovered through the painstaking collection of self-knowledge is every bit as legitimate as one that comes in a sudden epiphany. This less traveled road leads to the same destination. It is only when it is not taken because of the twists and turns and bumps along the way that we reach a dead end.

It is common to rationalize not doing anything about an unsatisfying work life with the argument, "How can I go out and find my ideal work if I don't know what I want to do?" This version of the chicken-or-the-egg question is merely a justification for standing still and an excuse to complain—which is why a colleague of mine who works at a prestigious business school tells the graduate students who come to her whining about not getting anywhere in their work search, "If you don't know what you want, it's not surprising you're not getting it."

There are three ways to find out about anything. You can read about it. You can talk to other people about it. You can try it yourself. Think of these as three successive stages you pass through before arriving at your ideal work. In stage one, you do some research, and then you ask yourself, "Am I sufficiently interested in this to talk to someone who is doing it?" If the answer is yes, you move to stage two, the information interview (see Chapter III). After an interview you ask yourself, "Am I excited enough about this to talk with someone else?" If after a number of conversations you are still engaged, you are ready for stage three—"How can I try it out."

At no point along the way is it necessary to ask yourself the big, often paralyzing, question, "Is this what I want to do for the rest of my life?" You simply focus on a series of next steps, working your way through the stages until you either realize that you're on the wrong track, in which case you start over with a different possibility, or until you arrive at a place that feels like home. It's like driving in heavy fog. You can't see your destination, but you can see a car length or two ahead, and after you've traveled that distance you can see a little further, and so on. Over time, the habit of exploration will result in a picture of a professional life that develops gradually, like a Polaroid® photograph—first as a blur, then as vague shapes, next as recognizable objects, and finally as a clear image of the work that you, with your own personal collection of skills, experiences, and idiosyncrasies, were meant to do in this world.

Career Autobiography

There are countless ways of collecting self-knowledge, but more important than any particular one is the act of honoring the things you learn about yourself by writing them down, sharing them with others, organizing them into some meaningful form, and regularly revisiting the picture as it unfolds. By documenting, communicating, structuring, and reviewing your insights, your growing self-knowledge will produce something tangible from a farrago of formless thoughts.

When I was writing resumes, I discovered how much it means to people to have the chance to tell the whole story of their professional life. Most conversations about work go something like, "What do you do?" "I'm an X," and that's the end of it. My clients found it exhilarating to be able to talk about their work life in detail.

A career autobiography is a free-form narrative that covers your education and work-life from the beginning. It is radically different from forcing your history to fit the mold of a resume. The resume is a formal exercise with a *fixed external purpose*, getting a job. A career autobiography is an informal exercise with an *evolving internal purpose*, self-knowledge which supports authenticity. Writing it provides a chance to flesh out the bullet points of your resume and include the backstory. There is no right or wrong way to go about it, but there are few things to keep in mind.

Begin at the beginning.
A resume presents the most recent events first and moves backward in time. A career autobiography starts at the beginning, when and where and how you grew up, and moves forward in time (though it may contain flashbacks, digressions, speculations about the future, etc.)

Set the stage and fill in the background.
Position yourself within the context of your family, your education, the cultures of the places where you worked, etc. For example, "I

94

come from a middle-class family with two older sisters. My mom stayed home and my dad worked for the same company for twenty-five years. General Electric was almost a member of the family."

Relax.
This is not going to be published in *The New Yorker*. It's for your eyes only, so don't be afraid to make it informal. Pretend you're talking to a trusted friend over coffee or writing a letter to someone you've known for a long time.

Pause to take stock.
At turning points in your story, stop and ask yourself what influenced your decision and what was going on inside you when you made the choice to take the path you did.

Look for themes and patterns.
If you write something like, "I took the job, despite the long commute, because it meant I would be able to build the program from scratch," try to identify where the notion of building something from scratch comes from, why it's important, and where it shows up in other places in your life.

This list is by no means intended to be exhaustive, nor are these hard and fast rules. It is merely intended to provide a framework to help you explore your story. Do what feels most comfortable. If writing comes easily, put down everything you can think of, and then go back and highlight what stands out, and prepare an edited version to share with others. If writing is difficult, record the most pertinent facts in outline form. Walk through your professional life as if you were taking a tour through a historical building, and record highlights as you go. If even this seems too daunting, have a friend interview you on tape, asking you a few simple questions such as, "Tell me a little about yourself. Why did you decide to major in X? What did you gain from that experience at Y? What did you like most about Z?" Listen to the tape and make a note of what speaks to you.

Once you have gotten your autobiography down on paper using whatever method works best for you, find someone to tell it to who will listen attentively and *quietly*. Avoid well-meaning family members and friends who may feel compelled to comment or make suggestions. You need a patient listener who will not distract you, because in the course of telling your story you're going to say things that *you* need to hear, and you don't want to miss them. That's the real purpose of doing it.

A skilled counselor is an excellent choice. It has the added advantage that you will be providing the background the counselor needs to help you achieve your career goals. If you are not ready to use a professional, telling your story to a friend or colleague will yield some of the same benefits and start you off in developing the essential skill of articulating who you are and what you have to offer.

The career autobiography is an overview. The next step is to examine in greater depth the moments in your life when you felt fully alive and completely enjoyed being who you are.

Peak Moments

We're accustomed to hearing the story of a professional life told almost exclusively in terms of outstanding achievements. Ask a Major League pitcher to reflect on his career, and he'll tell you about his no-hitter. Ask an actress, and she'll talk about her role in a hit movie. Ask a writer, and he'll recall that it was his third novel that lifted him from obscurity and made him a best-selling author. But what about the rest of us who've never won a Cy Young Award or an Oscar or a Pulitzer Prize? What are our peak moments?

A peak moment is simply a time in your life when you felt a deep sense of accomplishment and personal fulfillment over the part you played in some event. It may be something that the world knows about and applauds you for, or it may be known only to you and your family and friends. It doesn't matter. What's important is the sense of personal fulfillment. Recognition, or the lack of it, is fundamentally irrelevant.

In fact, it is often true that the less world-shaking the experience, the more valuable it is on a personal level. On a resume you can say that you successfully negotiated a million-dollar contract or implemented a just-in-time inventory system that saved the company $300,000 a year. You can't say that you cared for a dying parent or mentored a troubled teenager through to graduation or helped to set up a neighborhood watch program, even though these things may have provided greater satisfaction.

By identifying, writing down, and telling the stories of your peak moments, you are "mining" your career history, and as you dig deeper into old shafts that seemed played out or open up new ones, you discover the skills you most enjoy using like gold nuggets or precious gems. Taking a close look at those times in your life when you put forth your best efforts *measured purely by your own standards* is the foundation upon which you can build a professional life in which what you do is an expression of your authentic self.

Guidelines for Skills Stories

I am indebted to Richard Bolles, author of *What Color is your Parachute?* for the story-writing exercise that follows. His spirit continues to serve as an inspiration for my mission.

Step One: List Peak Moments.
Think back over your life, and try to remember anything you did which was meaningful to you in a personal way. Use what Bolles calls a "memory net"—review your history in terms of places you lived, schools you attended, jobs you held, etc. Some people find it helpful to proceed a decade at a time. Use whatever approach seems most natural to you. The goal is to be as thorough as possible.

Step Two: Choose Topics.
From your collection of peak moments, select six to ten to write about. They can, and should, include everything, from selling potholders door-to-door at the age of ten to winning a Salesperson of the Year award, from earning a music merit badge in Boy Scouts to playing in a professional symphony orchestra. The topics you choose should represent the full spectrum of your life. Don't focus just on your career. Try to select at least one topic from your pre-career days, and at least one that represents something you feel you've lost track of along the way.

Step Three: Write Up Each Topic In Narrative Form.
Tell what happened, your part in making it happen, how the outcome affected you and others, and why the accomplishment is meaningful. Focus on content rather than form. This is not a literary exercise but a mining expedition, and the goal is self-discovery, not polished prose. Most people can tell a story in a page to a page and a half, and if you find you need more space, you may be trying to tell more than one.

Step Four: Mine Each Story for Skills.

Between the lines of what you have written are the skills you most enjoy using. Now you need to identify them. To do this, reread your stories looking for evidence of what there was about you that allowed you to accomplish the goal or overcome the obstacle. Then share your stories with at least two other people, and ask them to identify the skills they see there. Often their list will reveal abilities that come so naturally to you that you don't think about them. As you continue your skill-collecting, you will find that the same ones come up again and again. These repeated patterns point to the "motherlode" you're after, the skills you most enjoy using.

The interests, experiences, abilities, dreams, fantasies, and wild ideas that emerge from these stories are the raw material of a new professional life. The next step is to see what you can make out of it. You sort and organize your findings in whatever way makes sense to you, without prejudging what ultimately may or may not be useful, and then you keep playing with them, like a jigsaw puzzle, until they start to come together.

Piecing it All Together

In sharing her stories of peak moments with trusted friends, Carla, a marketing communications consultant and business writer, heard a different kind of energy in her voice whenever she spoke of her extra-vocational interests—history, design, and quilting.

She decided to pursue them by doing volunteer consulting for a historical site and teaching quilting to Girl Scouts. These experiments provided her with an opportunity to spend time with people in a world she had never been exposed to before, and as one project led to another, she came to see how the skills that had served her well in business could be applied to non-profit organizations. After all, writing a proposal wasn't really all *that* different from writing a grant.

In time she discovered a number of career possibilities that related directly to her interests, and she wrote them down on color-coded scraps of paper and arranged them on a "vision board" similar to the design wall she uses to test out quilt patterns and color combinations. She paired her current expertise with the contrasting colors of the new skills she was learning and organized everything around the focal point of work that would be more creative and satisfying.

Her current design is a mix of "purples" (quilting guild president, dealer, appraiser), "yellows" (writer of family histories, grant writer, corporate communications consultant), "blues" (marketing consultant to non-profits, teacher of sewing classes) and "oranges" (silent partner in a fabric shop, non-profit board member).

Her collecting and sorting have allowed her to incrementally shift her focus to the things that excite her while staying grounded in the professional skills she has already accumulated. The new combinations are helping her to piece together a whole range of career options she would never have imagined.

Organizing Self-knowledge

There is work you are meant to do, and work you are not meant to do. There is work which calls for skills you enjoy using, and work which calls for ones you don't enjoy. There is work that leaves you fulfilled and energized, and there is work that leaves you drained and empty. Discerning which is which requires time and energy, but if you don't do this, you could face the dilemma of, to paraphrase Joseph Campbell, having the ladder you are climbing up against the wrong wall.

We naturally establish criteria for the things we buy. For example, if you're going to purchase a car, you at least have some idea of what you're looking for before you go to the showroom, e.g., color, gas mileage, leather seats, etc. Why shouldn't you do the same for the work you "buy" with your time, energy, and dreams? Having a set of objective specifications provides a standard for evaluating opportunities which significantly reduces the risk that your emotions will affect your decision or that you will talk yourself into something which isn't a good match. It also serves you well in shaping how you do the work and the terms you negotiate, so that when you receive an offer you can say, " 'Yes, I'll do that. But this is the way I should be doing it. This is the way it should be structured. This is the way my relationships should be. These are the kinds of results you can expect from me, and in this time frame, because this is *who I am.*' " (Peter Drucker, *Management Challenges in the 21st Century*)

There are many tools to help you articulate, group, and prioritize your specifications into a "first draft" of the next chapter of your professional life, one that will continue to be edited and revised as you accumulate more self-knowledge. The gold standard, Richard Bolles' "Flower Exercise," is described in Appendix A.

How do you move from, "I don't know what I want to be when I grow up," to "I am the person to do this work"? The short answer is, intentionally and incrementally, by practicing disciplines that move you closer to I-am-the-person certainty and make what you have to offer more attractive and looking for work less stressful. In the post-workquake world, where change is constant and mobility the norm, this is not a "touchy-feely" exercise which the serious business professional can slough off or attend to only sporadically. It's a business necessity.

If you're thinking, "I don't have time to fool around with this, I have bills to pay," you should know that the "hard" pursuit of traditional job-search at the expense of the "soft" work of knowing yourself is actually counterproductive in the long run. Why? Because an employer looking to hire someone is always going to favor the person he believes will do more with the job than just get it done. Regardless of the task, there is an aura of the *craftsman* about the person who brings to his work a joyful alignment between it and himself.

Today the market for work is a buyer's market. How do you stand out? How do you make yourself visible? The answer is simple but not easy—by knowing exactly what you want to do and why you are the person who is ideally suited to do it. If the purchaser of a service (i.e., an employer) can pick and choose from a large pool of candidates, then authenticity is a competitive edge, one that may well be decisive.

CHAPTER VII

Work the Problem

The process of becoming a leader is much the same as the process of becoming an integrated human being. For the leader, as for any integrated person, life itself is the career. Leadership is a metaphor for centeredness, congruity, and balance in one's life.

Warren Bennis and Joan Goldsmith
Learning to Lead

Life is always to be tackled anew.
Carl Jung
The Structure and Dynamics of the Psyche

Much of the action in Ron Howard's 1995 film *Apollo 13*, about the NASA mission to the moon of April, 1970, takes place not in outer space, but on the ground in Houston, where a large cast of geeky characters responsible for a meticulously designed flight plan monitor the rockets, power usage, life support, guidance systems, etc. from Mission Control. Each has his own function in a large, complex piece of organizational machinery, and all are highly skilled at carrying out a mission that has been mapped out down to the smallest detail.

The flight is going well, until there is an explosion aboard the spacecraft 200,000 miles from earth. The engineers leap into action to respond to a plethora of warning lights and alarms, but it soon becomes evident that their emergency procedures are not only of little use, they are actually making the situation worse. One of them looks at his monitor in disbelief and says, "This can't be happening." Yet it is.

At this point, Flight Director Gene Kranz holds up a thick book and throws it away. "I want you to forget the flight plan," he says. "From now on, we are improvising a new mission. Let's work the problem, people." Stop thinking about how it's supposed to be, he tells them. Don't guess at what might happen. Stay rooted in the task at hand, and take one challenge at a time.

Kranz's leadership does for the Apollo 13 flight what we must do for ourselves if we are going to claim the ground of our own choosing—define reality, reshape the mission, work the problem. We *define reality* by taking a hard look at what's really going on and being honest with ourselves about what isn't working any more. We *reshape the mission* by envisioning what a new professional life could look like. Finally, we *work the problem* by moving toward realizing that vision one step at a time.

Self-leadership is critical for the work-seeker today because he is dealing with transition on two fronts, one personal, and the other global. The world of work he is part of has experienced its own change event, the workquake, thus he is in transition on both a micro and a macro level. He has the choice of enduring this grudgingly or using it as a means to professional transformation. If he opts for the latter, he places himself within the context of something far more meaningful than just getting the next job. By choosing to utilize the creative space as an opportunity to better align who he is with what he does, he will become more authentic, marketable, and whole.

The point of choice, where the Ground of Your Own Choosing is either claimed or abandoned, is often prompted by what appears to be a disaster, such as the loss of a job or the threat of it, or it could be triggered by the general angst and confusion that everyone is feeling as a result of the workquake. Yet these difficulties also contain the seeds of a new freedom to break out of the way we've always done things and respond more creatively. When our preconceived notions of how to proceed are stripped away, we can access the power within ourselves that allows us to transcend self-imposed limitations. It is then that we are ready to commit ourselves to "work the problem," understanding that this may require making things up as we go along. The story of Apollo 13 provides a perfect analogy.

As a result of the explosion on board the spacecraft, the landing on the moon is scrubbed, and it's questionable whether the crew will make it back alive. The three astronauts are forced to abandon the main part of the spacecraft and use the Lunar Excursion Module as a lifeboat. The problem is that the LEM has been designed to support two people for a day and a half, not three people for the four days it will take to return to earth. The filters which remove carbon dioxide from the air inside the module quickly become saturated, and the astronauts are in danger of asphyxiation. There are extra filters available, but they are square and the receptacles on the LEM are round. For the astronauts to survive, the Apollo 13 engineers have to figure out how to fit a square peg into a round hole. They gather up a collection of things known to be available on board the spacecraft—a space suit, some hoses, a roll of duct tape, plastic bags, etc. Then they dump it all out on a table and proceed to see what they can make out of this jumble of stuff. The solution they come up with in working the problem is nothing like what they would have designed under other circumstances, but it works. And it's ironic that the flight plan plays a pivotal role—not for its content but for the outside cover, which becomes part of the contraption they fashion to allow square filters to be used in a round receptacle.

In working this problem, and a multitude of others that arise, the engineers go far beyond what even they would have thought they were capable of. No one understands the energy and creativity they demonstrate better than Flight Director Gene Kranz. When one of the NASA executives remarks that Apollo 13 could be the greatest calamity in the history of the space program, he retorts, "With all due respect, sir, I believe this is going to be our finest hour."

Here are some examples of ways that people have been able to reach their "finest hour" by working the problem in their professional lives.

Working the Problem I: The Grounding Statement

Joyce had been restless in her position as a manager with a medical software company for some time. She had a vague sense that something was missing in her work, and when she did her own "job satisfaction rating," she gave it only a 50 percent. A short time later, when she started to notice signs that the company was imploding around her, she took a closer look at her situation and realized that she was more than dissatisfied—she was in trouble .

Because she understood that jobthink had landed her where she was, she was open to trying something new. Her first step was to identify and describe the things she wanted in her work that weren't there. By writing short narrative accounts of peak moments in her life (see Chapter VI) and mining these stories for the conditions under which she had thrived and the skills she most enjoyed using, she came to see that she had lost the sense of being connected to making people's lives better through her work.

She did an in-depth analysis of her earlier roles in healthcare, looking at the organizational cultures, the qualities her supervisors had valued in her, and the qualities she had valued in them. Themes and patterns began to emerge, and she was able to target the human welfare issues she most cared about. Research provided a list of organizations which matched her interests, talents, and abilities, and information interviewing (see Chapter III) helped her to refine her vision and narrow her sights to specific roles she would consider. Over time, she was able to move from the vague notion of doing "something" for a non-profit organization to the idea of being an Operations Manager or a Program Officer for a healthcare foundation. She also defined her requirements for compensation, placing a premium on quality-of-life issues, especially around the length of the commute because of the pressure it might put on her as the mother of young sons. She figured the low end of the range based on an ideal commute, and a high end based on longer travel.

She compiled all of this information into a one-page Grounding Statement (see Appendix B for a sample Grounding Statement) which she used to renew professional relationships she had allowed to languish and initiate new ones. She sent it first to people she knew and respected, asking for their suggestions. Later she distributed it, along with a letter of introduction, to the professional contacts of family members who worked in human services.

One of the responses she got back directed her to a women's health institute close to where she lived. She applied for and got a position there as an administrative manager. Her resume played a part in this process, but a very small one. It appeared late in the game, and only as a formality. Had she used it prematurely, it would have shut down the exploration. A resume asks for a job, and if there is none available, the conversation is over. Joyce's Grounding Statement simply asked for information, and her questions fed the process of making the right connections.

Working the Problem II: The Targeted Bio

Anne was on a fast track to a Director of Marketing position with a Fortune 100 company when she learned she was going to have a baby. Personally she was thrilled, but when she thought about its effect on her career, it felt like a professional disaster. Even before the pregnancy, the demands of her work left her exhausted at the end of the day. She missed simple things, like having time for exercise, preparing healthy meals, visiting her family, all of which were very difficult to fit into a fifty-plus hour a week job with a long commute.

While she was on maternity leave, she started to reclaim some of the things she missed, and by the time her son was born she had already decided she didn't want to return to work full-time.

Her first act of self-leadership was to negotiate a part-time position, which was unprecedented in her company. The exercise gave her practice in speaking her truth, articulating her vision, and staying in a lengthy, step-by-step, negotiation process.

The part-time role gave her the freedom to explore other options. She was drawn to the idea of building a consulting practice which would allow her time with her son. Since she wasn't quite sure if this was right for her, she decided to test it out by doing a project for a friend who owned an advertising agency.

Later, through a neighbor, she made contact with the managing partner of a consulting firm, and when he asked her for a resume, Anne was faced with a choice. Should she position herself as a potential employee? Or should she operate from the ground of her own choosing?

Instead of a resume, she responded with a one-page targeted bio (see Appendix B for a sample), outlining those aspects of her experience which she felt would be most relevant to the company's needs as she understood them. She asked for a face-to-face meeting, and in the meeting she focused on communicating and substantiating her experience in strategic planning, business development and team-building, areas where the company needed help. The managing partner liked what he heard and asked her to submit a project proposal.

She didn't feel she knew enough to put together a proposal and price it appropriately, nor was she sure how involved she wanted to be with this company, so once again she countered with something different from what had been requested, a plan to survey their needs so that they could better understand how to utilize her services and she would have enough information to know if she wanted to continue working with them.

Her leadership initiatives convinced the managing partner not only of the soundness of her ideas, but also that she was the right person for the company to establish a relationship with. By positioning herself as an expert, not a jobseeker, and engaging in dialogue with the company on a peer-to-peer level at its cutting edge, she changed the conversation completely and established a precedent for setting her own terms. Plus, she was able to carry off her exploration within the parameters she set for having time with her son. Now, instead of her career being set back by becoming a mother, it is moving forward.

Working the Problem III: Letter-Writing Campaign

After receiving his degree in economics, Phil accepted a job as a financial analyst. At first it seemed like a good fit, but within a few months, it ceased to look so promising. He was bored and wanted to do something creative.

For a couple of years, he tried to construct the job he wanted within the framework of the job he had. He initiated a number of projects—a product spinoff, a video, a book proposal—yet for various reasons they never got off the ground. There was little support from management, and he always seemed to wind up back in the same place.

A generation ago, someone in Phil's situation might have said, "I don't want to waste twenty years doing this." It's an indication of how things have changed that Phil was saying, "I don't want to waste *five* years doing this." He quit the job and started looking in the usual way—newspaper ads and Internet job postings. He looked at opportunities in journalism and radio, searching for something that would provide a creative outlet, but the only response he got was from companies who needed his financial skills. He didn't expect a miracle, but he did hope to get closer to finding fulfillment in his work.

The primary reason for his struggle was that his vision of what he wanted was still undeveloped. He knew he was looking for "something" with growth potential in an industry where innovation was possible. He wanted to believe in and be moved by the work he did, but he couldn't be more specific than that. He needed a clear goal and a plan for achieving it.

Intensive work with a career professional helped him to trust his instincts and develop his ideas into a strategy. The Strong Interest Inventory® enabled him to identify those areas in the real world which aligned most closely with his interests and values and narrow the possibilities so that he could explore them in depth.

His refocused job-search now ranged far beyond the traditional approaches. He used his writing skills to make contact with people in the fields that most interested him, starting with letters to alumni from his college. A diligent campaign of correspondence (see Appendix B for a sample marketing letter) led to information interviews, and as time went on, he found himself drawn to advertising because so many of the people he admired were working in that field. Through his community of contacts, Phil began to get job interviews, and because of all he learned through information interviewing, each one was a "slam dunk." He got three offers for jobs in advertising account management, and he was able to call upon his network of people within the industry to help him assess and evaluate them before he accepted the one from a large agency in New York.

Phil is hopeful for the future, but he knows that if for some reason the job doesn't pan out there's no need to worry because he has made himself the master of a work-search strategy which will be there for him when he decides it's time to move on. He also knows that he has a community of people who will support him every step of the way when he does.

Working the Problem IV: Targeting Organizations

While he was a salesman for a company that tested electronic circuits, Walter figured out a way to offer the service at a lower price, and he used it to establish his own company. The business was an immediate success, and after eight years he was able to sell it for a considerable sum. Part of the agreement required that he remain with the company for one year after the sale. It turned out to be a hard year for Walter. He was forced to watch as the new owners ran the company he had founded and nurtured to success into the ground.

When the year was up, Walter got work selling financial services, and did extremely well—so well, in fact, that his boss felt threatened and began to sabotage his efforts. He moved to another firm, and once again the same thing happened. Six months later he left, angry and discouraged. He found himself out of work with two kids approaching college age. He was spiraling down into depression, and his wife and friends were beginning to be concerned about him.

For Walter, working the problem began with some serious soul-searching. He recognized that in order to move forward he had to put aside some of his bravado and acknowledge that, after three body blows in a row, what he needed was something that would help him begin to restore his confidence. Rather than aim high, which was what he had always done, he would have to lower his sights and find work that was *safe*. The best place to do that was somewhere he already knew the culture and the politics, where he was a known entity and would not be blindsided. The obvious choice was one of the non-profit organizations whose boards he served on.

For many years, Walter had been very active in his community, and his volunteer work and charitable giving had resulted in his being invited to serve as trustee for several organizations. It was clear that in the non-profit world, the area of fundraising offered the best fit for his experience and qualifications, so he set out to learn as much as he could about it. After a number of information interviews (see Chapter III), he was speaking the language of development like a native, and the more time he spent with people in the field, the more his confidence grew. His background in sales made him very good at cultivating relationships and asking people for money, which was what it was all about.

When a development opportunity opened up at the hospital where he served on the board, he was ready to go for it. Rather than submitting a traditional resume, which would have listed his community service activities at the bottom, if at all, he put them on top where paid work experience usually goes (see Appendix B for a sample), and he wrote cover letters detailing how his community service was directly related to the achievement of development goals. His resume documented the re-engineering of himself. It didn't drive it. From his years of involvement with the hospital, he knew all the players and had a firm grasp of the lay of the land, so it was easy to find people who would support him as a candidate. Six months after his period of despair, Walter restarted his career as a Major Gifts Officer for the hospital. Within a year, he was promoted to Chief Development Officer, and few months after that, Executive Director.

Dumping Out and Reconfiguring

Like the Apollo 13 engineers, these individuals were all faced with working the problem of making a square peg—their experience, skills, and talents—fit into a round hole—an opportunity. They started by "dumping out" the content of their professional lives and taking a look at everything that was there. They sorted through it, organized it, played with it, put it together in different ways, until they were able to reconfigure it into something that fit. They stayed at it long enough, despite stress and discomfort, to turn their assets and attributes into an advantage. They chose a creative solution rather than the application of formulas and worked the problem rather than following a preset plan. The solutions they came up with may not have been exactly what they thought they would be, but they worked. And in facing the challenge, these people took their creativity to a new level.

Too often people faced with a disaster in their professional life try to cling to the plan, hence the perpetuation of jobthink. Yet through self-leadership—defining reality, reshaping the mission, and working the problem—they can begin to find or create the work that meets

their criteria. Whether they do this on their own or enlist outside resources doesn't matter. What's important is the willingness to make
themselves accountable for operating from the ground of their own
choosing.

CHAPTER VIII

Your Inner Entrepreneur

Entrepreneurship is a mindset . . . . The trick is to educate and encourage the largest number of people to feel comfortable with the notion that they can start a business, control their destiny, and contribute to society through their innovation and hard work . . . . Our goal is to make starting a business as common as getting married or parenting.

Carl J. Schramm
The Entrepreneurial Imperative

Shifting the responsibly for creating work from "them" to "you" is not a simple change. It requires effort, learning, and patience, but with the decision to make your career security dependent on yourself also comes the potential for greater professional freedom and enjoyment. This empowerment begins the moment you place yourself at the center of things by thinking of every encounter with a source of work as an opportunity to communicate how you can benefit them. When the objective of connecting what you have to offer with the needs of the workplace drives your actions, you will have gained the status of a business resource providing a service, rather than a jobthinker looking for somewhere to re-attach the umbilical cord. Then you will be able to engage in business-to-business dialogues and not be subjected to the often discouraging and sometimes humiliating person-to-business protocols that govern admittance to a organization as an individual. You won't be just one of thousands applying for a position, making telephone calls that aren't returned, sending emails that aren't answered, going on interviews and waiting for a response.

Melissa had been a graphic artist with the same publishing firm since she finished college. She was a hard worker, and although she received regular praise from her boss, she didn't feel that the company valued her. She hadn't been promoted, and for several years the only pay increase she got was a yearly cost-of-living raise. She knew from conversations with colleagues that she was underpaid, but she dragged her feet on doing anything about it because she was petrified at the idea of having her work critiqued by strangers.

The need for additional income eventually drove her to put together a portfolio and start looking for another position. Her first interview was in a corporate headquarters of majestic proportions. She navigated a complex color-coded route to the appropriate underground garage and arrived at the reception area a little frazzled. She looked around and wondered if this cold, cavernous architectural wonder had been designed just to intimidate her and make her feel small. If so, it had succeeded.

A security guard directed her to the corridor where the elevators were, and as she stood there looking at her reflection in the polished black marble, she grew anxious about being late, about her portfolio, about her professional abilities, about her very existence on the face of the earth! She was so wrapped up in feelings of insecurity that she literally jumped when the security guard tapped her on the shoulder and told her she was facing the wrong way, the elevators were behind her.

The art director asked to see her portfolio, and she watched in agonized silence from the other side of the desk as he flipped through the pages, hardly glancing at her best work. He gave it back to her without comment. The experience was so demeaning that it was weeks before she could get up the courage to try again, and when she did, the same thing happened. She was getting nowhere, but more importantly, her confidence in her abilities was being badly shaken. She had to find a way to protect herself.

Her situation began to improve when she decided she was going to reframe her search by considering each encounter with a hiring manager as a business-to-business exchange. She went to her next interview *as if* she were an agent calling on a client to offer the services of an artist who happened to be named Melissa. She walked into the art director's office with the attitude, "I am Melissa's representative, and it's my job to take charge of this meeting and make sure you see that part of her portfolio which is most relevant to your needs." In order to do this, she had to find out about his current projects, so she spent the first part of the interview asking questions. When she felt she had enough information, she sprang to her feet and turned to the appropriate pages in her portfolio with, "Based on what you've told me, I think you'll want to take a look at this, and this, and this." To her delight, he did.

When the search for work is viewed as a business-to-business activity, the playing field changes dramatically. By presenting herself not as a subordinate but as a peer, as one business talking to another, Melissa accomplished three things.

First, she was able to be strategic in the conversation and come off as a confident, self-actuated resource.

Second, she protected herself from the "poor little me" feeling she had by the elevators at the first interview. She wasn't there to sell herself, but the services of her company, "Melissa Graphic Arts, Inc." What was at stake was not her worth as a human being, but the performance of her business in *just this one encounter.*

Finally, by lessening the emotional cost, she discovered that she could be reasonably comfortable in a meeting. Consequently, she will do more of them, increasing the likelihood that she will find work that is more rewarding.

There has never been a time in history when you could be a business of one and compete as effectively as you can today. Technology has leveled the playing field, and being small actually gives you the advantage of being able to respond faster to change. Power is passing from the large organization to individuals who are willing to accept it.

Diane was a software engineer for the same company for many years. She liked the work and was comfortable there, and when the company started showing indications of being in trouble, she put off taking action, hoping that her longevity, plus her track record of glowing reviews, would allow her to get by until things began to turn around. It didn't, however, and she was let go.

Soon after she was laid off, a former boss who had moved on to another company offered her a consulting position, and she took it. She enjoyed consulting, and it met her financial needs, but since she had become self-employed not by choice but by a combination of necessity and luck, she was still mired in jobthink. Whenever she spoke about her situation to friends or colleagues, she talked as if it were an temporary inconvenience she would have to put up with until a "regular job" came along. She couldn't even bring herself to call it by its right name, self-employment.

In *The E-Myth Revisited: Why Most Small Businesses Don't Work and What to Do About It*, Michael Gerber observes that every small business owner must fulfill three roles—the Entrepreneur, who creates the vision of what the business can be; the Manager, who organizes and structures that vision into a plan; and the Technician, who performs the tasks necessary to implement the plan and bring the vision to fulfillment. Ideally a business should be a balanced blend of these three, but Diane's business was closer to 85 percent Technician, 10 percent Manager, and only 5 percent Entrepreneur.

According to Gerber, businesses fail because the people who start them are Technicians who set out to create a *job* for themselves, not a business. They prefer to devote their energies to whatever their expertise happens to be, and their focus is on production and operations, not vision and organization. They fail to understand that the "technical work of a business and the business that does that work are two totally different things."

Whether it's a business or a career, when the Technician dominates,

Entrepreneur	Technician
Strategy	Tactics
Cultivating new opportunities	Getting the work done
Innovation	Routine
Focus on the sale	Focus on the thing sold

the focus is on tactics, not strategy. What's important is getting the work done, not cultivating opportunities to grow. The energy goes to the task at hand, whether it's making widgets or tweaking a resume, and new ideas are seen as distractions. There is no place for thinking outside the box and experimenting with ways of reinventing oneself. Innovation is stifled and jobthink replaces the process of connecting to and satisfying the marketplace.

One day Diane was complaining to a friend who had been a consultant for many years about how stressful it was not to have a secure future. The friend got fed up with her grumbling and said to her, "Get over it. A lot of us live this way all the time. It's called self-employment!" Hadn't she learned anything? Her former job could hardly be called a sure thing, yet she had held on to it for dear life. And by relying on her current consulting assignment as her sole source of work, she was setting herself up for the same thing to happen again.

It was a wakeup call. Diane had to admit that her situation was precarious. She had no backup plan in case she should lose her consulting gig, and if that should happen, this time she would be without even the modest protection of severance. That's when she started to get serious about developing her inner Entrepreneur and Manager. She started to envision what she wanted her consulting practice to look like in three years, five years, ten. She took courses in business development. She became active in professional organizations and cultivated a community of relationships she could call upon for support. Through her contacts, she was asked to take on several short-term moonlighting projects. Recently one of them has opened up an opportunity for future work, more than she can handle alone, and she is now thinking about subcontracting other consultants.

Diane's story is a wonderful illustration of what Cliff Hakim notes in *We are All Self Employed: How to Take Control of Your Career*: "Successful people are working two jobs: one is the position they hold in their daily lives, and the other is self-leadership of their work life."

It's All Business Development

A few years ago there was story on the PBS *News Hour* about a program designed to teach people how to be entrepreneurs. In itself, this was not surprising since many colleges, in recognition of our changing times, have added entrepreneurial programs to their curricula. But this was not at Harvard or Stanford. The students in these classes were inmates at Riker's Island, the largest jail in New York City. "We've got to change their hustle," explained their instructor. "If no one is going to hire them, they have to be able to hire themselves. We teach entrepreneurial skills today because tomorrow there will be no jobs."

A similar situation exists on outer Cape Cod where I live. Because there are no large companies and very few year round jobs, the local economic development council offers a program to teach people the basics of owning a business. For the last ten years I have been closely involved with this program, both as a developer and a presenter, and I have learned a great deal about what happens to people as they work through the process of becoming an entrepreneur.

In the beginning, it's a struggle for them to accept that *running* their business is going to require a lot more than just working *in* their business, and they will have to become proficient in a whole new set of business development skills. When they realize this, they usually either dig in or bail out. Those who stay with it seek out as much business development education and training as they can find and start to build an infrastructure of people they can trust to take on responsibilities they feel ill-equipped to handle. Watching the progression of these nascent entrepreneurs, it has become unmistakably clear to me that the ones who make learning a priority and stay connected to others who are in the same boat have greater success and enjoy business ownership more.

Everyone who is looking for work, whether it be self-employment or job-employment, should spend some time in classes like these, because all work-search is business development. Trying to find work as a computer programmer or a marketing executive is fundamentally no different from starting an insurance agency or opening a catering service. The same business development skills are required for both, and acquiring and honing them is as critical to long-term success as any job skill, because no amount of professional expertise *by itself* is going to bring work in the door. Just being good at what you do is no longer enough. Now you need to think, speak, and act like the CEO of your own company. What a person does to make a living falls under the category of business operations. What he does to make it possible for him to do this work comes under the heading of business development, and there can be no business operations unless business development comes first.

Jim was a star performer in a Chicago law firm. He and his wife made the decision to move back to the town where they both grew up because they wanted to raise their children in a rural community close to family. It wasn't long, however, before Jim began to feel stifled by the small family-owned law firm that hired him. He decided it was time to think about hanging out his own shingle, but before he could do this, he had to create a foundation for presenting himself as a business entity by asking himself the following questions:

What are the market conditions that create this business opportunity?
Jim's personal desire to get out on his own, passionate though it may be, is not enough by itself. He will have to back it up with solid market research that demonstrates a need for a law practice that specializes in estate planning.

What business am I in?
Jim will no longer be able to simply say he is an attorney. He will have to articulate his mission in a way that expresses what makes it unique—in his case, a holistic approach to end-of-life issues.

How do my services solve problems, achieve favorable results, or improve upon what's currently available?
To answer this, Jim will need to learn about the needs of the over-fifty-five population of the community through research and information interviewing. He can then use the data to target potential clients and sources of referral.

Why am I the right person to do this?

The answer to this question is *not* a one-minute elevator pitch, but the story of how and why Jim came to see the legal profession as his calling, starting with the moment as a young man he first heard the phrase *Counselor-at-Law* and decided it was a way he could make a difference in the lives of others.

What is my product? How it is priced? What is my plan for promoting it? Distributing it?

Jim will have to develop each component of his marketing plan and understand how they are interrelated. For example, he may decide to distribute information about ethical wills (product) by offering presentations in libraries (distribution) free of charge (price) because it is an effective, low-cost way to advertise his business (promotion).

What are the benefits my clients receive from what I have to offer?

Jim is very adept at explaining how the legal documents he prepares can protect his clients from probate costs, but he will also need to be able to speak to the psychological and emotional benefits—peace of mind, passing assets and values on to the next generation.

How will I continue to survey the marketplace and revise my business plan?

A business plan has been aptly called the story of a business in words and numbers. It is not a static document but a narrative that continues to unfold. Jim will need to continue to collect information about his customers, marketplace, and competitors and revise his business plan accordingly.

These business development questions are applicable to any work search. If you are looking for job-employment, this exercise in thinking through how to market yourself *as if you were a business* will help you to substantiate what you have to offer in business-to-business conversations and become fluent in articulating your professional value from the Ground of Your Own Choosing.

Sustaining Your Entrepreneur

People starting out in business come to it full of excitement. They are energized by the thought of giving birth to something new in the marketplace, whether it's turning used oil from restaurant deep-fat fryers into biodiesel or operating a bakery that makes dog biscuits. They glow with anticipation of how they will be able to deliver a better product or service to their customers and improve upon the offerings of their competitors. They are full of visions for the future and see endless possibilities: "Maybe in a year or two I could expand my product line, sell to wholesale as well as retail markets, open a satellite location . . . ."

They have the same sense of amazement I once saw on the faces of my son and daughter-in-law as they looked down on their month-old first child kicking happily on a blanket on the beach. Struggle and disappointment, which inevitably come because nothing worth having is ever perfect or effortless, haven't yet started to chip away at the awe they feel about their new creation.

Regardless of whether we work for ourselves or someone else, we have to find ways of re-experiencing the enthusiasm that originally led us to do what we are doing. I do this by grabbing a legal pad and getting out of the office to a coffee shop or the park, someplace where I can see the business as something apart from me. There I simply play with new ideas and ask myself questions like, "What would I like to do more of?" Unless I periodically give my full attention to the entrepreneur in me who is responsible for the strategic direction of my business, I run the risk of having my business starve because I'm not doing anything to feed the dream. There is a well-known proverb which states, "Where there is no vision, the people perish." It also applies to business. If you aren't able to access the entrepreneur within you, you're in trouble. Work without a vision for the future, a sustaining purpose, and opportunities for innovation devolves into drudgery.

The entrepreneur lives in a world of what-ifs and why-nots. He asks himself questions like:

- What would my work look like if I freed myself from its constraints? What would I do if I could do whatever I wanted?

- What if I could make my work truly unique?

- How could I do what I do differently?

- Who could I talk to who might help me expand or clarify my thinking?

- How would I act *now* if I knew I could achieve what I'd like in the future?

- How can I satisfy my customers' thirst for new products and services from the springs of my own creativity and initiative?

In answering these questions the entrepreneur takes responsibility for giving life to the future of his work. He knows that nothing can become a reality unless he believes in it and communicates it in a way that others can understand it, because no one else is going to want it unless he does. Even if his vision lies far beyond his current circumstances, it's still there to be relied upon, like a landmark a sailor uses to get his bearings at sea.

When actor John Lithgow (*Terms of Endearment, Third Rock From the Sun*) was an undiscovered talent making the rounds in Hollywood, he was a long way from being the Shakespearean actor he had dreamed of becoming. What he did, however, to keep his dream alive eventually led to its fulfillment. The entrepreneur in him established a group of actors that met regularly to read Shakespeare together.

In the beginning it was just him and a few others who loved the Bard with enough scripts to go around and a six pack or two. With Lithgow's urging, they met consistently for the purpose of putting into their world what they felt was missing, a chance to act in something more meaningful than a razor blade commercial.

Over time, word of Lithgow's Shakespeare group spread to directors and producers, and Lithgow ended up in effect branding himself as a Shakespearean actor. He recently played Malvolio, the comic villain of *Twelfth Night,* to rave reviews at the Shakespeare Theater in Stratford, England.

Lithgow's story is an excellent example of what can happen when someone starts to ask himself, is there something positive I can do instead of pounding my head against the wall? How can I structure my world to include what I really want? What if I surround myself with people who share my passion? By acting as if he already was a Shakespearean actor, Lithgow became one.

Whatever your professional aspirations, learning to play the leading role in developing them will take you to the Ground of Your Own Choosing.

CHAPTER IX

Selling Yourself

*Courteous people with backgrounds in clerical work make
better information providers and problem solvers with
today's smarter customers than the stereotypical aggressive, outgoing sales types of the past . . . . They are willing
to answer questions and patiently let customers come to
their own decision.*

> Harry S. Dent, Jr.
> *The Great Jobs Ahead*

Before the workquake, it didn't matter if you'd rather hang by your thumbs than sell. Today, however, changes in the workplace mean that sales will be a part of your professional life whether you like it or not. Even if you don't have sales responsibilities added to your job description, as some will, you will be expected to contribute to the revenue flow by serving customers inside or outside the organization. In addition, the trend toward shorter tenures means that you will have to go out and sell yourself to a new employer every three to five years.

While there is no way to escape becoming proficient at sales, this doesn't mean that you have to be a master manipulator like Ricky Roma in the David Mamet play, *Glengarry Glen Ross.* In fact the opposite is true. It will be your ability to make genuine connections and keep your attention on the other person's agenda rather than your own that will make you effective.

Good News/Bad News

The tax accounting service that Sarah established after she became an Enrolled Agent supported her for a number of years, but then came the ready availability of tax preparation software on personal computers and competitive pressures she felt ill-equipped to deal with. She has tried to revitalize her business by adding bookkeeping and debt counseling services, but the results have been disappointing because, as she says, "I'm just not a salesperson." She is discouraged and considering closing her business and starting to look for a job.

Sarah assumes that she has to be a certain type of person to be effective at selling. This may have been true at one time, but it no longer is. The same seismic changes that created the workquake have also turned the nature of sales upside down. The educated consumer has made the hard sell ineffective, and the aggressive type that comes to mind for most people when they think of sales—a type many of us are not and have no desire to be—is becoming an endangered species. The car salesman who tries to razzle-dazzle you by manipulating the numbers or talk you into buying the car he has on the lot instead of the one you want is wasting his time when you can get on the Internet and find out everything you want to know about any make or model, including price and availability.

He is being replaced by people who were previously behind the scenes in support roles because they are the ones who know how to access and communicate the information customers need to make good buying decisions. The solo voice is giving way to backup singers who are able to sing in harmony with the consumer. This is a kinder, gentler way of selling in which the people who know how to get things done actually have an edge over those who depend on hype and fast talk. It works whether you're trying to sell merchandise to a customer, a service to a client, an idea to your boss, or your qualifications to an employer, and because it doesn't depend on any personality type, almost anyone can master it.

That's the good news. The bad news is that Sarah no longer has an excuse not to sell. In fact, even if she does close up shop and look for a job, she will still have to sell herself to an employer.

Yet the news is not so bad if she realizes that all that's required of her is that she be well-informed, make herself available, and conscientiously follow a few simple steps to build and sustain relationships. This is a set of business skills that anyone can develop, not a magic touch that some people have and some don't. It isn't necessary for Sarah to learn how to work a room, but she will have to replace her fear of being innately inept with a commitment to gaining competence and comfort in the discipline of selling herself.

Consultative Sales

Old-style sales is about results. In a business context, that means closing the deal. In a work-search, it means getting an offer. If you score before the buzzer rings you win. If you don't, you lose. That kind of pressure to perform can produce anxiety in just about anyone.

Consultative sales is about establishing relationships. If old-style sales could be compared to winning the championship, consultative sales would be more like building good stats over the course of the season. What matters is not the outcome of any one particular game, but how well you do over time. Consultative sales has nothing to do with pitching, pressuring, or scoring. Its cornerstones are connection, dialogue, and patience.

- *Connection* is about meeting the other person where they are, rather than imposing your agenda on them. You enter their world respectfully, not forcefully.

- *Dialogue* is about a balanced exchange in which both parties contribute equally. Information flows in both directions and the conversation is not scripted.

133

- *Patience* is about trusting that good things come in unexpected ways when we make connections with a lack of urgency and conscientiously nurture them.

The important thing is not what the person on the other side of the desk does or does not do, but how well you handle yourself in each interaction. By taking your stand on the Ground of Your Own Choosing and paying attention to the things you have control over, you access an inner authority that makes whatever you are trying to sell more attractive. This quietly radical approach invites you to let go of worrying about outcomes and concentrate instead on making yourself known as a valuable resource and trusting that over time this will brand you as a go-to person.

Arlene was just this type of go-to person in the family-owned bank where she worked. Over the course of her sixteen years there, she developed a number of strong relationships with customers. The owners had come to recognize her as a valuable asset, but when they told her that in order for the bank to remain competitive she would be required to sell, they almost lost her. In her mind, Arlene associated sales with "being pushy." She thought she would be required to talk the customers she had done business with over the years, many of them friends and neighbors, into accepting things they didn't want or need, and this was totally at odds with her image of herself as a trusted resource. Fortunately the owners were smart enough to bring in consultative sales training to help Arlene and the other Customer Sales Representatives understand that between the one extreme of aggressive hustling and the other of just being nice there was a third option—providing information and education to help customers make buying decisions which were in their best interests.

In a consultative sale, both sides look at a problem and craft a solution together. Imagine a woman shopping for a washing machine in an appliance store. The salesperson who approaches her doesn't try to overwhelm her with a litany of features or pressure her to take advantage of a limited time offer. Instead, he asks her what she's looking for, and when she tells him that she doesn't know, there are so many choices, he asks if she's concerned about the environment. When she says she hasn't considered the environmental impact of her choice, they talk about wastewater problems in the area where she lives. The salesperson provides her with information about a washing machine which uses less power, water, and soap and tells her how to apply for a fuel efficiency rebate. She buys the machine, actually spending more than she had planned, and leaves feeling good about her decision.

Work Search As Consultative Sales

The consultative sales approach is invaluable for people who are engaged in work-search, whether they have been laid off or have chosen to go out on their own. After all, work-search *is* sales, and many people, like Sarah, who find themselves thrown into it feel out of their element. Yet they can be effective and comfortable if they pattern their work-search on the consultative model which is rooted in values that are easier for them to get their arms around. For that reason alone it is a better choice for work-searchers. It has the advantage of protecting them from two negative repercussions of standard sales practices—rejection, and the loss of authenticity.

Mary was a community leader in a popular tourist destination. She became interested in the growing movement of green tourism, and the more she learned about it, the more she wanted to find a way to sell the tourist organizations where she lived on the idea, but she was apprehensive about being rebuffed by people she had known for many years when she approached them for paid work. However, she did feel comfortable with being visible at tourism events, and she took it upon herself to keep the local leaders in the industry up to speed on what was happening in this hot new field. Soon they began to recognize her as an expert, and they invited her to consult with them on several green tourism projects. She never had to face rejection because at every step in the process she conducted herself not as a salesperson but as a valuable resource.

In consultative sales, the work-seeker views an opportunity to talk with a potential employer or client, not as a chance to make a sales pitch, but as a two-way conversation to explore mutual benefit. Some would say this approach takes longer, but having to pick yourself up again and again after being rejected is also time-consuming, not to mention the toll it takes on your confidence. Whether you're presenting yourself as a potential employee, or as a consultant, or a vendor, a strategy that buffers you from rejection is obviously better because it allows you to stay in the process.

Not so obvious as rejection, but just as damaging, is the fact that the traditional sales approach to work-search blunts your competitive edge by obscuring your authentic self. Adopting a persona that isn't you is like putting on a bulky overcoat. It covers up the lines of the finely tailored clothing underneath, and it's so awkward you can't move around in it very well.

If your work-search isn't compatible with your true self, you will not be able to present the best of who you are. And like rejection, compromising your authenticity will make it harder for you to stay with it. Whether it's a garment or a behavior, if it doesn't fit, you're going to shed it sooner or later. You will simply stop putting yourself out into the marketplace because it's too uncomfortable.

A consultative sales work-search is a bit like dating. You meet, you talk, you find out what you have in common. As you continue to learn about each other, a connection grows, or it doesn't. Pretending to be someone you're not doesn't work. The goal is to build relationships, not play games.

Consultative sales really isn't sales at all. It's marketing. You listen to what the other person needs, and then you present yourself as a resource for meeting those needs. You do this by showing genuine interest, making helpful suggestions based on solid knowledge, respectfully maintaining a dialogue, and completing each cycle of communications, including closure, when necessary.

Show Genuine Interest.

Being genuinely interested in another person requires a spirit of openness and a sincere desire to understand what is important to them. It has its own rewards, whether or not it leads immediately to an opportunity. You may not think anything happens, but later on you may find that the person you talked to becomes a source of information or a link to someone else.

Author and television host Art Linkletter once told the story of an insurance salesman who called on him every year for twenty years. They always had a pleasant conversation, and the man never stayed longer than ten minutes. Linkletter never bought insurance from him, but he did refer many others. They had such a good relationship that when he didn't show up one year, Linkletter phoned his office to find out what happened. The salesman had had a heart attack.

People know when someone has been attentive and they value it. They also know when they're being hustled, no matter how well it is disguised. Asking open-ended questions starting with interrogatives like *who, what, when, where,* and *why* is a good way to show you're involved in the conversation. It will usually lead to a more detailed response than a question that can be answered with a yes or no. This shouldn't be part of a calculated plan to bring about a certain outcome (what salespeople have traditionally called a "yes-train") but a way of helping someone clarify their needs. Because the goal is to maintain a dialogue over time, there's no hurry to make your case. Indeed it is often far better to carefully evaluate a person's answers before responding. "Let me think about what you've said and get back to you after I've had a chance to do a little research," is a perfect way to show genuine interest.

Make Helpful Suggestions.

To be seen as a resource, you must present yourself as one, even if only in small ways. To do this, you make suggestions based on the information you have. The more information, the better you will able to match what you have to offer to a set of needs.

The office where Darren works is closing, and within a few months he will be laid off. During his tenure with the company, he developed on his own initiative a system of internal communications which greatly improved productivity at his location, and other offices within the company have expressed an interest in it. Darren is thus in a perfect position to go to the company and propose that they hire him as a consultant to implement his system company-wide and train staff in its use. Darren has trouble thinking of himself as a salesperson, but he is not at all uncomfortable with the idea of presenting this as a "helpful suggestion" because he knows it's in the company's best interests to take him up on it.

You could think of this as a kind of matchmaking—fixing up a need with a solution. In using the knowledge he has as a company insider to make recommendations, what Darren is doing is not really all that different from what Amazon.com does when it tells you about products you might enjoy based on ones you have ordered.

Maintain Dialogue.
Maintaining a dialogue lies at the heart of consultative sales, and following up after a meeting is the first step in keeping the conversation going. There are many ways you can do this—direct conversation, indirect reference through mutual friends and associates, cards, letters, emails, a newsletter, are just a few examples. When you make the decision that you want to cultivate a relationship with someone, you are responsible for developing a communication plan that answers the following questions:

- How often do I want to be in touch with this person?

- Will I communicate regularly (i.e., monthly, quarterly) or spontaneously when something brings the person to mind?

- Will my communications be extensive or brief, detailed or cursory?

- What sorts of things will I discuss?

- What method(s) of communication will I use (i.e., email, telephone, face-to-face conversation)?

- What criteria will I use to determine whether the relationship continues to be fruitful?

- At what point do I move on?

Gordon submitted an idea for a column to the editor of a business journal, but because he didn't know enough about the publication's mission, his proposal missed the mark. However, he really liked the editor and thought he could learn a lot from working with him, so he decided he would stay in touch by writing to him once a month for a year. In each letter he tried to pass along something that was happening in the business community he thought the editor would be interested in. He also let the editor know about what he was doing and reiterated his interest in writing for him. There was no response, but then out of the blue the editor called and asked him to write two articles. For eight months, the communication had seemed one-sided, yet all along they had been in dialogue.

Complete Each Cycle of Communications.
A consultative sales meeting has three parts: preparation, meeting, and follow-up. Every interaction should follow this complete cycle.

Follow-up is the backbone of relationship building. It's a business discipline that transcends sales and a practice that with diligence can become second nature.

Gina was very good at her job as an administrative assistant in a large company, but she hated the corporate environment. She loved being outside and would rather work with animals than most people. She got interested in training guide dogs for the blind and was excited to find a place that did that not far from where she lived. She went to an open house at the training facility and met the director of the program and the person in charge of the canine development center where puppies were bred, and the conversations went well because Gina had done extensive research beforehand. Because there was little turnover, there wasn't much hope a position would become available for her in the near future, but the director was open to having her stay in touch. Gina then put her administrative skills to work by setting up a schedule for maintaining regular contact. Not long after she began her campaign, Gina got a call from the director. One of her employees was getting married and was leaving unexpectedly. Gina was the first person she thought of to replace her.

Sometimes completing the cycle means executing some form of closure. You will need to clean house now and then to close out connections that have not proved to be worthwhile. If there are people in your contact database who are non-responsive, it is far better to close the loop by taking a final action (i.e., making a last call or sending a closure letter) than to allow feelings of rejection to weigh you down. Many times people decide they are not good at sales simply because they have not learned how to let go of people who don't call back.

CHAPTER X

Professional Self-Care

[The] feeling of being valuable is the cornerstone of self-discipline, because when one considers oneself valuable, one will take care of oneself in all ways that are necessary. Self-discipline is self-caring.

M. Scott Peck
The Road Less Traveled

If one sets aside time for a business appointment, a trip to the hairdressers, a social engagement, or a shopping expedition, that time is accepted as inviolable. But if one says: I cannot come because that is my hour to be alone, one is considered rude, egotistical or strange . . . . Actually these are among the most important times in one's life—when one is alone. Certain springs are tapped only when one is alone.

Anne Morrow Lindbergh
Gift from the Sea

The decision to take your stand on the Ground of Your Own Choosing and say with self-assurance, "I am the person to do this work," is a courageous one, and like any act of bravery, it will naturally be accompanied by feelings of vulnerability and fear. Stretching ourselves emotionally increases the demand on our energies, and under pressure our capacity to perform can become compromised, just as an electrical power grid is taxed during a heat wave. Replenishment from external sources is indispensable if we are to keep moving over the rough patches of self-doubt. A safety net of support, new learning, and time spent in quiet reflection, are integral to the Ground of Your Own Choosing, because this is how the strategic, creative, and innovative behaviors on which it depends are accessed. If we don't continually refill our reservoir of ideas and possibilities, the demands of daily life will suck it dry.

Marsha was Vice President of Marketing for a consumer products company when she came to me for a career retreat (see Appendix C for more on career retreats). She was desperate to do something about her sixty-hour work week and restore a sense of balance and professional well-being. She had been aware for some time that the demands placed upon her were eroding not only her quality of life but also her effectiveness as a leader. What she did not see was that she had cut herself off from the professional nourishment that had made her successful in the first place.

After reviewing her impressive career track, I asked about the people who had helped her along the way, her teachers, mentors, role models. For a few moments, her face went blank as she groped for names, like searching for something recognizable in a dense fog. I asked how often she accessed these nurturing voices and when she had last had contact with them, and she slowly shook her head. She had been too busy, and the busier she had become the more she had isolated herself, until the relationships that had given sustenance to her professional life had slipped away. She had all but forgotten what it was like to spend time with a trusted colleague and be fed.

I was sitting across the table from an accomplished, highly-paid, well-dressed executive. How strange that I should be reminded of Edward Steichen's *The Family of Man* which shows a collection of photographs of starving people from Holland, India, China, and the Arctic, with the caption, "Nothing is real to us but hunger." Marsha's work had taken her over so completely that nothing was real to her but her hunger to get out of the situation she was in.

I see some degree of professional starvation in almost every client I meet with, and what they are starving for is professional renewal.

In an essay entitled, "Effectiveness Must Be Learned" (*The Es-*

144

sential Drucker: The Best of Sixty Years of Peter Drucker's Essential Writings on Management), Peter Drucker observes that when we refer to some part of a business as a "profit center," we are using a "polite euphemism." Profit comes solely from outside the organization, or as he wryly puts it, "The only profit is a customer whose check hasn't bounced." Inside the organization, he says, "There are only cost centers," the drain of resources necessary to produce a product or a service.

The same principle applies to individuals. While it's true that working hard makes us productive, it's also true that it uses up the creative energy we need to assure our professional security. If we are going to remain on the ground of our own choosing, we will have to find ways to replace it. Just as a general, no matter how skilled or gallant, can't win battles unless his army has the provisions it needs, a campaign to find or create meaningful work can't succeed without a supply-line of self-care.

Marsha began to re-supply herself by getting in touch with a former boss who had mentored her in an earlier stage of her career. She reconnected with colleagues in her industry she had lost track of and made a commitment to maintaining regular contact with them, no matter how crazy her travel schedule got or what demands were pressing upon her. These people became her lifeline to the outside world, and through them she began to see that there were possibilities other than what she was doing. They gave her a vision beyond her current circumstances, and later, when her division was sold, and she was given the choice of losing her job or taking a lower level position, they were there to help her use her considerable business knowledge and marketing experience *in her own behalf* to find new channels of work.

Core Circle of Support

No one reaches the ground of their own choosing alone. To get there and stay there you need help. One of the best ways to do this is to form what I call a "core circle of support." These are people you select by asking yourself, just as any leader would, "Who can best help me accomplish my goals?" Most likely the individuals you choose for your core circle will already belong to the larger circle you have constructed through community-building (see Chapter IV). They will be the ones with whom your relationship has deepened to the point where you are comfortable sharing with them your whole story—the truth about why you left your last job, or your innermost fears about being held back because you don't have a degree. You trust them enough to feel safe venting negative emotions or testing out half-baked ideas.

The core circle serves as a kind of personal advisory board. Its purpose is to keep you moving toward your vision by making you accountable for taking the next action and not allowing you to give in to negativity. You'll still fall off the path from time to time—it's unavoidable—but with the help of a core circle you'll get back on it quicker and lose less ground.

A core circle is a mix of mentors, advisors, colleagues, friends, etc. who respect your abilities and want you to succeed. Here are a couple of examples:

- For her core circle, an educational consultant has chosen a former professor, a business coach, several peers who share her enthusiasm for professional development, and a maiden aunt who simply adores her. Each person provides a necessary component of support: the professor has the knowledge to direct her to the right people, the coach is working with her to professionalize her business, friends feed her enthusiasm and stimulate new ideas, and her aunt provides a welcome cup of tea when she's had a tough day.

- The senior partner of an executive coaching firm has built his circle from organizational development thought leaders he has gotten to know, a clinical advisor he meets with regularly to review challenging cases, the head of a non-profit organization with whom he shares a passion for professional growth, classmates from a leadership training program, and a friend from high school who owns a charter fishing boat and provides respite on days when it's too beautiful to stay cooped up in the office.

Creating a core circle of support is a simple idea, but it requires a commitment to keep the people you have selected up to date with what is happening to you and inside you. Unless you make an effort to communicate with them regularly, they can't be of real service to you. Only you can provide the information and continuity of contact that keeps your circle alive and strong. The head of a corporation has regular conversations and meetings with the members of his board. As a Ground of Your Own Choosing work-seeker, you will do the same, except that you will be doing it as the head of a business called My Professional Future.

New Learning

I have a clear memory of the day I put my oldest daughter on a school bus for the first time. It's an experience I relive every September when I see kids congregated at the bus stop at the end of the street where I live. You don't forget how frightened and small your child looks climbing aboard a big yellow bus that is taking her away from you. I can still see her bravely walking toward the steps in a new dress and shiny shoes, biting her lip and clutching a Flintstones lunchbox.

Going off to school, whether it's to first grade or college, is a clearly defined rite of passage in our culture. Where we often fall short in our thinking, however, is in not acknowledging the value of learning *throughout* our lives. Whether we are five or nineteen or thirty-six or sixty, it's not easy to get on the bus, but it's essential to our continued growth that we do. By moving out of a comfortable, known world into a larger unknown one we expand our capabilities.

Paul is a technology consultant who thrives on challenges others won't touch. He loves what he does and does it well, and clients are naturally attracted to him because of his knowledge, enthusiasm and integrity. The downside of this is that he tends to make himself too available to too many people. There aren't enough hours in the day for him to get done everything that's on his plate, and as a result he has slighted his own professional development.

An opportunity came up for him to attend a strategic technology conference at a prestigious university, and he very much wanted to go, but he knew that if he did he would not be able to meet a project deadline for one of his most important clients. It was a difficult decision. Should he focus on getting the work done, or should he feed himself? He chose the latter. He dreaded having to tell his client that he would not be able to finish on time, but in the end, he was able to convince him that this was a once-in-a-lifetime learning opportunity, and ultimately they would both benefit from it. He returned from the conference full of energy and ideas. In getting away from the nitty-gritty, day-to-day operations of his business and immersing himself for a week in "the rarefied air of the ideal," he found a whole new direction. Experiences like Paul's are mini rites-of-passage which we create for ourselves by seeking out new learning experiences among people with credentials different from our own.

A career education plan that includes both formal instruction and self-study is essential to maintaining the vitality of your work-life. Here are a few suggestions:

- Imagine you are taking courses in a graduate studies program, and create your own "syllabus" of readings on various topics. One "semester" you might focus on leadership, the next on marketing best practices, etc. If you find yourself underlining every other sentence in one of the books, get on the Internet and find out when and where the author is speaking or conducting a training and consider making an investment in your professional development by attending.

- Ask for recommendations from people who are in a position to give you feedback about the education or training valued in the markets where you want to find work. For example, Steve was a photographer who wanted to get into multimedia. He thought he would have to go back to school for a computer science degree, but when he talked with the Director of Marketing of a company he had done work for, he found out that a certificate program from a design school was actually looked upon more favorably.

- Ask people you respect and admire what kinds of education they have most benefited from. When two or three people make the same suggestion, particularly if they are members of your core circle, you can be comfortable that it's something worth considering.

- After attending a learning venue presented by a thought leader whose philosophy aligns with yours, assign yourself a follow-up project. Offer to pass along what you've learned to your colleagues through a "brown-bag seminar," or write a newsletter article. Nothing reinforces learning more than teaching or writing. The practice of forcing yourself to apply in some concrete way what you have learned assures it will become part of your professional life, not just a line item on your resume or a binder in your bookcase.

- Keep learning about yourself, your strengths, weaknesses, blind spots, bad habits, etc. Continue to refine your understanding of how and where you are best able to contribute. Peter Drucker developed a method for this he called "feedback analysis," based on ideas that Jean Calvin and Ignatius Loyola incorporated into the rules of life for the communities they established in the 16th century. In essence it works like this: whenever you make a major decision or take an important action, write down what you think will happen. Then six, nine, or twelve months later, look at the result of your decision or action and see how it compares to what you expected. This simple discipline will help you direct your time and energy to areas where you excel. The fact that Drucker, the "bard" of business writers, practiced this for over twenty years and was always surprised by it, speaks to its power.

There is a big difference between using a learning opportunity to discover your authentic self and enhance your value in the marketplace, and throwing education at a career problem, e.g., the person who goes to graduate school after finishing college because he can't find a job or is not sure what he wants to do. It doesn't solve anything. It just means he doesn't have to think about it for a couple of years.

I once spoke to a class of MBA students, full-time working professionals who had decided to pursue an advanced degree in order to progress in their careers. I started my presentation by asking them how much time they devoted to their jobs, and the responses ranged between forty and fifty hours a week. I asked how much time they gave to their studies, and they answered ten to twenty hours a week. Then I asked how much time they spent managing their careers, and at first there was silence, then nervous laughter. Finally someone said, "Not much." I told them that the MBA they were working so hard to earn wasn't going to benefit them unless they could communicate its value to someone in a position to reward it, and *that* was a career management task.

Just as it's necessary to make sure your ladder is against the right wall (Campbell) in your work life, the training or education you undertake needs to support well-defined goals. Information interviews (Chapter III) with people who have pursued a particular form of education you're interested in help to cross-check whether it's appropriate for you. Regardless of the educational venue, you are a *customer*, and you have the right as well as the responsibility to find out if the learning you are considering purchasing with your money, time, and dreams is going to help you reach the Ground of Your Own Choosing.

Time Away—Short Pauses

Lowell, Massachusetts, is widely regarded as the birthplace of the Industrial Revolution in America. Much of downtown Lowell is now a national historical site, and if you go there you can visit the Boott Cotton Mills where thousands endured the hardships of factory work from the beginning of the nineteenth century through the early years of the twentieth. The men, women and children who worked in the mills went to work when the bell rang at first light, and they left twelve to fourteen hours later, depending on the season, when the bell rang again to mark the end of the day. It was backbreaking work, yet it came to an end when the sun went down.

No such limits exist in the Information Age. The mind-numbing labor goes on 24/7. As harsh as life was for the mill workers, they had something we do not have—a clear beginning and end to their working day *set by someone else.* Now it's up to the individual to decide when he or she is done for the day. Just as the power harnessed from the Merrimack and Concord rivers which converge in Lowell made the textile industry possible, the power of the microchip has made it possible for us to work anytime, anywhere. But the fact that we are able to extend our working day into commuting time, evenings, holidays, and even leisure activities, does not mean we have to, nor does it mean that it's in our own best interests.

Trying to make good use of the portability, flexibility, and convenience that electronic devices offer *without* losing the renewal space we need to live balanced lives is a challenge. You can begin by becoming aware of when you allow work to bleed over into the non-working part of your life. This doesn't mean that you never cross the line between the two, only that you know where the line is. Without such consciousness, it will become so indistinct that you won't be able to see it at all.

Any practice that helps you be clear about when you are working and when you are not has value. Turning work off is as much a discipline as returning messages, preparing for a meeting, or any other business practice. Here are some suggestions:

Block out "sacred spaces."
Designate some part of your day, a mid-morning break, fifteen minutes after lunch, the first thirty minutes after you get home, that belongs only to you. Use these sacred spaces for some renewal activity like reading, looking at art, getting outside, exercising, taking a nap.

Create "no-phone zones."
If cell phone companies can "roam," so can you. You might choose to use your cell phone only during working hours or when you are traveling on business. Designate times of day or locations where you don't pick up the phone because to do so would keep you from being present to yourself or another person. Reflexively answering the phone makes someone who isn't in the room more important than someone who is.

Practice the art of controlled availability.
Let people know when you are accessible so that you can protect the times you choose not to be. Tell your staff or your clients exactly when you will be in the office or responding to messages. By establishing these parameters you will also be telling them when you are *not* available. This will set a limit in a way that respects both their needs and your own.

Utilize transition rituals.
In earlier times, people relied on the bell or the sun to tell them it was time to stop working. We can create our own signals for the end of the work day. For people who work and live in the same place, changing clothes is a good way to make this transition. Those who commute could have a landmark on the way home—an exit, intersection, road sign—which they designate as a cue to stop thinking

about the office and start thinking about how they are going to spend the evening.

If we are not vigilant, work will bleed us dry. We need to keep our working selves and our living selves separate so that each can be strong enough to support the other. Like St. Louis, which straddles the Mississippi River between two states, Missouri and Illinois, we need to build an arch that symbolizes the fact that we have an identity on both sides of the river.

Time Away—The Strategic Vacation

I hear people talk about insane travel schedules, unrealistic performance expectations, unrelenting pressure from customers and staff members, etc., and then in the next breath they talk about an upcoming vacation as if somehow by magic it will make all those problems go away and not be there when they return. Holding on from vacation to vacation makes getting away not a source of renewal but a part of a cycle of self-abuse. All I can think of when I hear about people misusing vacations this way is an alcoholic who goes into a rehab to dry out, feels a little better, and comes out and drinks again. The dependence on periodic vacations to rest up from a persistent condition of overwork is not all that different. Eventually it will get to the point that even the most luxurious or exotic leisure destination will no longer do the trick. The fix will stop working.

On the other hand, when you think of it strategically, a vacation becomes an opportunity for discovering ways you want to live differently. It's not simply leisure. It has a goal, to hold on to some of what you learned while you're away so that you can integrate it into your non-vacation life. A strategic vacation is about reshaping your life for the long haul. Your success in bringing back a new insight or behavior which supports the accomplishment of something that is important to you—having fun with your children, writing a book, experiencing more peace and centeredness in dealing with the demands of your everyday life—is the principal indicator of whether vacation time has been used strategically as part of a continuum of self-care or as a stopgap in a pattern of self-abuse.

The more you try to accomplish in your life, the more important it is for you lock in time and space to restore your perspective, energy, and creativity. A retreat from the intensity of your "enterprise," whether it's self-employment or job-employment, benefits both you and your "customers," the people you serve, because meeting your business goals depends on your ability to deploy yourself fully, and you can't do that without replenishing your spirit.

Thinking of a vacation as a business decision helps you to remember that scheduling unscheduled time for rest and reflection is just as vital as any other business function because it allows you to capture the flickers of inspiration which get lost in the press of daily responsibilities.

Just as a field that has been allowed to lay fallow is more productive when it is replanted, time away yields an abundance of inner direction. For me, a strategic vacation to Gettysburg and a solemn walk up a hallowed field on a beautiful summer day resulted in a flash of intuition that connected the past to the present and ultimately led to this book.

In Conclusion

There is an old story that's been told many times by many different people. I first came across it in a wonderful book called *The Art of Possibility* by Roz and Ben Zander.

There are two salesmen who work for a shoe manufacturer. They are both sent to Africa to seek out new business opportunities. After a few days, one of the salesmen sends a text message back to the home office: "SITUATION HOPELESS THEY DON'T WEAR SHOES." A day or so later comes a text message from the other salesman: "WONDERFUL OPPORTUNITY THEY HAVE NO SHOES."

In adapting this story to my own purposes, I imagine two similar text messages, the first being, "SITUATION HOPELESS NO JOBS," and the second being, "WONDERFUL OPPORTUNITY NO JOBS."

The core meaning of the Ground of Your Own Choosing is epitomized by the second message. When external circumstances, especially the ones which feel like disasters, are thrust upon us, how we choose to respond is the *only* thing we really have control over, yet the choice we make has a profound effect on the outcome. This is what William James meant when he said, "by changing the inner attitudes of [our] minds, [we] can change the outer aspects of [our] lives." Which of the "inner attitudes" you choose, "SITUATION HOPELESS" or "WONDERFUL OPPORTUNITY," will determine whether you view the world of work from the valley of scarcity or the high ground of abundance where the advantage in creating a new, more fruitful, professional life is yours.

EPILOGUE

Last month the manuscript of my first book, *Ground of Your Own Choosing*, finally went to the publisher. You can't imagine the relief I felt to be approaching the completion of this intense, time-devouring project.

Putting your voice in the world in whatever form your creativity takes—writing a book, designing a bridge, developing a branding strategy—is exquisite agony. And how long it takes! My journey with writing began fifteen years ago in Bend, Oregon.

I was attending a training with Richard Bolles, author of *What Color is Your Parachute?* He was leading us in a skills exercise, encouraging us to think outside the box, and at the time I thought I added the word "writing" to my list of skills simply because I had a pencil in my hand and it was a handy response. Today I would be more inclined to see it as divine intervention.

Later, when I prioritized my list of skills, much to my surprise, writing ended up on top. I would have expected it rather to be public speaking or counseling which come much more naturally to me than writing.

After this experience I began to honor the act of writing in simple ways. I refinished my great-grandmother's desk so I'd have a special place to compose letters to friends and family.

Occasionally I wrote poems and essays, some of which found their way into the newsletter published by our church.

Being a contributor led me to the idea of creating my own newsletter which would force me to write regularly, and that's what I have been doing for the last five years.

To make the leap from newsletter to book, at the beginning of 2007, I committed myself to using my column as a venue for book chapters, one a month for a year.

The Inside Story

That is the linear, external version. Inside me, as I ran successive gauntlets of self-doubt, procrastination, and trying to figure just what it was I was trying to say, it was a lot messier.

The poems and essays I mentioned had only got written on long weekends because I didn't know how to give myself time to write, nor did I feel that my efforts were worth the investment. Writing was then a luxury which I could afford only after I'd cleared my to-do list, and unless I had a windfall of extra time, it didn't happen.

Even after my newsletter was being distributed to eager readers and I started receiving positive feedback, the idea of writing a book seemed totally unfeasible.

To offset my self-generated negativity, I found a writing teacher and mentor, and I spent several years in dialogue with her. She would sing a melody of direction and encouragement, and I would answer in counterpoint with all the reasons why I couldn't write more—a demanding professional schedule, elderly parents, children, grandchildren, community service commitments.

I'm tempted to say that "on paper" all of these excuses were real, but of course the issue was about not getting anything on paper. All of my justifications came down to my belief that I didn't have the time, which I now know is just an excuse for not being ready to commit myself fully to the creative process.

On the Train

To celebrate my 60th birthday, I traveled to Chicago on the Lake Shore Limited to participate in a program on "Transition in the Second Half of Life" led by William Bridges, another of my valued teachers.

My decision to take a long train ride rather than a short flight was a last-ditch attempt to impose a business solution on a creative problem, i.e., the book. The train would give me an expanse of time in which I could force myself to churn out an outline and few chapters to get things rolling.

This sounded reasonable, but it didn't work. I not only didn't write anything that came together in a way that made sense to me, I also got very angry at myself for failing to achieve my goal.

In the middle of the night on my return trip, with nothing to show for my Amtrak writing "retreat" but a page of illegible scribbling (which incidentally later became on of my favorite columns, see www.SuccessOnYourOwnTerms.com/newsletters/2005January. htm) I learned what I'd really come for—the realization that even my best business disciplines were not going to drive a creative process.

My forced march was a total failure, but by wanting to write enough to at least try it, I was able to break through an invisible wall and accept operating at the precarious edge of my own growth instead of relying on my known strengths. Thinking back, I realize that this was a wonderful example of a saying I heard recently: "Don't worry about falling—just lean into it so that when you fall you fall forward." Trying to mandate a solution to the book had caused me to stumble, but when I did I fell forward into a much better place.

After my experience on the train, the book became an internal rather than an external process. I stopped trying to get it done or figure out exactly where it was going. I'd spent months trying to come up with the perfect outline from which the book would "write itself," but ultimately the outline which proved the most helpful was a list of phrases from a brainstorming session I had had years earlier that I came across unexpectedly in a moment of frustration.

And Now That It's Almost Over

Although I can't say I have enjoyed my editor's insistence that I rework several chapters, or the seemingly endless revisions, I am beginning to see the value of being open to the synergy that comes from revisiting, reshaping, and refining with others what you thought was finished. This is something my "get it done" businesslike self (my MBTI® code ends with a very clear "J") finds very difficult to do.

By allowing the work itself to teach me how to do it, I gained something far better than the false security I had tried to create with file folders full of outlines and notes.

When in the despair of a blank period I would rummage through them—usually they were strewn all over the place because I no longer had the delusion that organizing my external space would be mirrored internally—I would find a comment or a snippet of information written years earlier which was still right on the mark, and it always came by accident.

The affirmation of seeing the core message of the book slowly materializing out of the rubble of five years of false starts was more comforting than any master plan I could have come up with.

A creative project requires a combination of discipline and looseness. In my fear-based attempts to build a rock-solid structure to support my writing, I had left no space for surprise, no room for the magic of pieces of the story coming together in unexpected ways.

By trying to orchestrate how it would happen, I took the energy and excitement which would invigorate and sustain my efforts out of the equation. Yet, without the discipline of establishing a regular writing time and a commitment to being productive, my efforts would not have gone much beyond wishful thinking.

Trying to strike a balance on the tightrope between will and creativity is ultimately an act of trust, not just that the project will somehow get done, but that by staying in the process you will become who you need to be to complete it.

APPENDIX A

The Flower Exercise

The purpose of the Flower Exercise in Richard Bolles' *What Color Is Your Parachute?* is to help you form "a picture of the job of your dreams" by listing your preferences in the following areas: places you'd like to work and live; things you're interested in; communities you wish to be part of; values; work environments; and compensation. Having done this, the next step is to prioritize each list using a tool which Bolles developed called a Prioritizing Grid.

I have adapted this strategy to my own practice by having clients create a list of work possibilities through brainstorming, research, information interviews, and assessment tools such as the Strong Interest Inventory®. Ranking their preferences helps clients to focus their energy on one thing at a time and keeps them from spinning in circles when new ideas pop into their heads.

I also recommend that they prioritize the skills that come up in Skills Stories (Chapter VI) and the qualities, both working conditions and interpersonal dynamics, which are important to them in a work culture, and use the results as a decision-making guide as work opportunities arise.

From using Bolles' Prioritizing Grid over the years, I have found the manual, paper version to be a bit cumbersome and error-prone, so I have developed an electronic version which is easier to manage. Readers who would like to use this version free of charge and with permission can access it from my website www.GroundOfYourOwnChoosing.com. There you will find detailed instructions on how to use the prioritizing grid, plus a sample prioritized list to get you started. You can use the tool to prioritize lists based on the categories in Bolles' Flower Exercise, or you can develop your own categories.

Sample Documents
(see Chapter VII)

Grounding Statement

Dear NAME,

Thanks for your offer to be a resource as I make my next professional move. I've always found personal connections to be the most effective and valuable way to navigate these kinds of transitions. Below you will find an outline of my professional skills, interests, and goals. Your responses to the specific question at the bottom of this document, plus any general suggestions or referrals you would like to make, will be greatly appreciated.

My experience has been in healthcare, though my professional/management skills are applicable to any field. My references are excellent. I have consistently excelled in:

- Communicating at all levels of an organization
- Managing and facilitating a team or project
- Needs assessment and program development
- Budget development
- Process re-engineering
- Working with customers/clients

I am currently a candidate for positions at X Medical School and Y Hospital. While I am open to these positions, I would like to explore other possibilities in other fields before responding to these opportunities.

165

I have been exploring working with an organization that makes a positive impact on issues I care about, such as:

- Women's health
- Children's health
- Literacy
- Parent training and development
- Human rights

I would be interested in speaking to any contacts you have in these fields. I also require: flexible work hours, a salary range between $ and $ and a good benefits package. Below are some of the roles I have considered:

- Program Officer in a foundation or corporate setting
- Program Director in a non-profit agency
- Director of Staff Development or Client/Customer Relationships
- Consultant for Relationship Management in a corporate setting
- Administrator at a children's hospital or clinic

In your opinion, would my skills be a good match with these types of positions? Can you suggest other roles that I should be exploring? As I navigate this transition, would you be open to continuing to be a resource to discuss ideas?

NAME, I appreciate your prompt response as this is an important decision-making time for me. Thanks for sharing your expertise with me.

Warm regards,

Joyce Smith

Targeted Bio

Anne Jones guides clients in the creation and growth of brands, whether they are for products or organizations. Serving clients in the manufacturing and service industries, she draws on 10+ years of brand management and sales experience which enable her to combine innovative strategic savvy with real word practicality. She has used this two-pronged approach to consistently drive business success across multiple venues.

Anne's ability to develop and prioritize strategic direction and to lead and motivate teams are key contributors to her success. She creates visionary, innovative plans that offer clients the opportunity to take brand growth to a higher level.

At the same time, her practical, focused approach enables flawless execution to ensure these opportunities are actually achieved. Throughout her work, she motivates those who are key to a project's success by acting as an effective team leader who fosters respect, drives autonomy, and inspires a common vision. Key aspects of her work process include:

- Defining clear objectives and goals
- Establishing and *inspiring* a cross-functional project team
- Applying realism in prioritizing and setting budgets
- Developing a detailed action plan
- Guiding plan execution to ensure success

Anne's most recent projects include: the long-term new product plan of a $400M consumer products brand, including defining the brand's core equity, and planning its extension via new product development; a business development plan to accelerate growth of a management consulting company.

Her expertise includes:

- Strategic Planning
  Annual Marketing and Business Development Plans
  Long-term Innovation and Product Life Cycle Plans
  Consumer Insight and Needs Analysis

- New Product Development
  New Product Idea Generation
  Product Concept Development
  Marketing Launch Plan Development

- Brand Messaging
  Brand Vision & Essence
  Key Messages & Claims
  Creative Strategy

Anne's client list includes X, Y, and Z. She has extensive experience in strategic brand management both in the domestic and global marketplaces for many different types of companies, including A, B, and C.

Marketing Letters

One of the most effective and underutilized marketing tools is the well-written letter. There is virtually no business development opportunity which cannot be advanced by it. A good letter begins a conversation by effectively presenting something of interest and value to the person it is addressed to.

To create an effective marketing letter, take a sheet of paper and draw a line down the middle to make two columns. Label the one on the left, "They Want," and the one on the right, "I've Got." In the left hand column, using a combination of factual data and brainstorming, list everything you think the individual receiving the letter would want in a person to do the work. In the right hand column, match each entry from the first column with one of your credentials using the language of your own experience. Place a star (*) by the credentials that best fit the work you are seeking.

Once you have completed this exercise you are ready to write a well-targeted letter. Start the first paragraph of your letter by turning the items you have starred into a statement of what most qualifies you for the work (e.g. "As a highly skilled career counselor, I have helped hundreds of people achieve their professional goals.") Use the second sentence in the first paragraph to substantiate the statement you made in the first (e.g., "My 25 years experience includes corporate outplacement, marketing expertise, small business consulting, etc."). In the second paragraph you will highlight some of the other selling points you have identified, and in the third paragraph you will state clearly the reason for writing and suggest a next step.

For example, when Phil began approaching advertising agencies his "They Want" and "I've Got" list looked like this:

They Want	I've Got
Strong sales skills*	Self confident presenter. Won public speaking awards in college. Highly developed verbal and written communications skills. *
The capacity to come up with new ideas*	Initiative in coming up with innovative projects (e.g. a spin off division, video, book proposal) for his former employer.*
Ability to deal with a challenge	Likes action and thrives under pressure. Goalie on winning hockey team.
Experience in account management	Efficiently handled a large portfolio of retail accounts in an earlier financial analysis role. Demonstrated attentiveness to details and follow up in these dealings.
Team Player	Knowing that others are depending him motivates him to succeed. This attitude began in his years as a goalie and continued in his work experience.

From these lists, he wrote the following letter:

Dear NAME,

I have the confidence and communication skills to effectively present myself to any client. These abilities served me well in my position with X where I regularly initiated creative projects, in addition to managing a large portfolio of retail accounts as a financial analyst.

My capacity to be a step ahead of what my clients needed and to attentively follow through on these requirements enhanced the performance of the merger and acquisition team I served on. Because of time pressures, the working conditions were often intense, but I enjoyed the challenge in much the same way I had thrived as a goalie on my college hockey team. Having others depend on me deepens my drive to succeed.

Through extensive research, which includes conversations with people in account management in a number of New York agencies, I have gained a excellent understanding of the account management role. This has confirmed that my skills and style would be highly compatible to a career in advertising. Several of my mentors in the industry have encouraged me to contact you, and I would welcome the opportunity to speak with you about opportunities at Y Agency. I will be in touch next week to arrange a convenient time to get together.

Sincerely,

Phil Smith

Resume Before "Re-engineering"

WALTER JAMES
10 Oak Lane, Kalamazoo, MI 49007
555-123-4567
walter@abc.com

QUALIFICATIONS

20 years of accomplishment and success contributing to businesses where I applied my exceptional interpersonal abilities and competence to educate and persuade. Utilizing my skills as a trusted advisor and problem solver, I excel at developing and cultivating clients, which results in a loyal customer following.

EXPERIENCE

Account Executive, PERFECT SOLUTIONS, INC., Kalamazoo, MI, 2003-present
- Sales of hardware and software solutions to healthcare industry.

Financial Consultant, FINANCIAL INVESTMENTS INC., Kalamazoo, MI, 1999-2003
- Ranked first for new accounts nationally every month since licensed in March 2000
- Developed 400 new clients
- Achieved "Blue Chip Council" status—highest award for new financial consultants
- Spearheaded seminar, "Foundations & Endowments," attended by 130 persons representing 60 different foundations

President, Treasurer & Founder, ACME ELECTRONICS, INC., Kalamazoo, MI, 1989-1999
- Founded electronic circuitry testing company with 30 employees— immediately profitable
- Recipient of "Outstanding New Enterprise Award"—Kalamazoo Chamber of Commerce

- Serviced large national firms and defence contractors
- Business sold to Milkitdry, Inc. in 1998

Sales Manager, CAPITAL TESTING SERVICES, INC., Kalamazoo, MI, 1987-1989
- Motivated and supervised staff of five salespeople

Sales Executive, UNITED CIRCUITS, Troy, MI, 1981-1987
- One of top 15 salespeople worldwide for division—achieved "Worldwide Legion of Honor"
- President's Roundtable—one of six to advise executive manage ment on improving products, services, and workplace environment

EDUCATION
B.S. Business Administration, Michigan State University

COMMUNITY SERVICE
Board member, Kalamazoo County Chamber of Commerce and various community and charitable organizations.

Vice President, 1990-1997, *Chapter Member of the Year,* 1992, Association of Digital Circuitry

Resume After "Re-engineering"

WALTER JAMES
10 Oak Lane, Kalamazoo, MI 49007
555-123-4567
walter@abc.com

Highly talented relationship-builder with exceptionally strong development and sales skills and a demonstrated commitment to the support of community resources, highlighted by: national and international top sales awards in every position held, a leadership style that attracts key players to the table, and proven ability to act upon bigger picture thinking.

RELATED EXPERIENCE
President, 1998 to 2005
Vice President, 1996 to 1998
Board Member, 1991 to 1996
ST. MARY'S HOSPITAL FOUNDATION, Kalamazoo, MI, 1999 to present

Natural leadership, history as an engaged volunteer and personal giving resulted in progressive responsibility for supporting the financial platform on which the hospital's mission depends during a critical period. Contributions include:

- Active involvement in all facets of fundraising and events promoting the hospital, including co-chairmanship of the golf tournament for 6 years during the formative years of the event when the expansion of corporate sponsorship was required.

- Full participation in a Capital Campaign, including identifying and securing commitment from leadership category donors. Counseling and assistance in developing planned giving strategies from which the hospital benefited.

- Enlargement of the "family of St. Mary's" through personal enthusiasm shared with a vast network of business and community contacts, including the active recruitment of 6 board members from a greater cross-section of the business and professional population.

Recognition as a bridge builder between the hospital's governing committees, the board and hospital personnel and the hospital and the community. Includes maintaining a highly visible presence in the community as a spokesperson and advocate for the hospital.

Financial Consultant, FINANCIAL INVESTMENTS, INC., Kalamazoo, MI, 1999-2003

- Talent for developing trust based relationship resulted in attraction and 100% retention of clients during very difficult financial market conditions.
- Ranked first for new accounts nationally every month since licensed in March 2000
- Developed 400 new clients
- Achieved "Blue Chip Council" status, highest award for new financial consultants
- Spearheaded seminar, "Foundations & Endowments," attended by 60 different foundations

President, Treasurer & Founder, ACME ELECTRONIC, INC., Kalamazoo, MI, 1989-1999

- Creative marketing strategies and high quality of workmanship resulted in national accounts in first year of business and reputation for client retention that attracted industry attention and the lucrative buyout of this firm that tested electronic circuits
- Founded electronic circuitry testing company with 30 employees— immediately profitable
- Recipient of "Outstanding New Enterprise Award"—Kalamazoo

Chamber of Commerce

- Serviced large national banks, insurance companies, and government institutions
- Business sold to Milkitdry Inc. in 1998

Sales Manager, CAPITAL TESTING SERVICES, INC.,
Kalamazoo, MI, 1987-1989

Sales Executive, UNITED CIRCUITS, Troy, MI, 1981-1987

- Motivated and supervised staff of five salespeople
- One of top 15 salespeople worldwide for division—achieved "Worldwide Legion of Honor"
- President's Roundtable—one of six to advise executive management on improving products, services, and workplace environment

EDUCATION

B.S. Business Administration, Michigan State University

APPENDIX C

The Career Retreat

What Is a Career Retreat?

A career retreat is about taking stock, regrouping, taking a close look at your professional life. It is space to re-evaluate where you are and where you want to go, who you are and who you want to be professionally. For many, regardless how long they've been working, it represents the first time they have accessed self-discovery resources, explored possibilities, and learned how to manage their professional lives.

Why Do it?

Taking time apart in a setting conducive to gentle introspection and blue-sky thinking can provide just the right environment for moving in a new direction. Examining patterns, exploring choices and learning new tools expedites the process of:

- Exploring career options
- Prioritizing life/work balance
- Dealing with change
- Orchestrating a career transition
- Gaining competence
- Mastering career management skills
- Moving from job-employment to self-employment
- Starting or enhancing a business
- Defining retirement goals
- Shaping or reassessing your business identity
- Developing self-marketing skills

The Retreat Process

All retreats are individual. Each is customized to the specific needs and circumstances as determined in an in-depth screening interview. Retreats are one or two days long with extensive preparation by the participant. Prior to attending, an agenda is developed and a pre-work packet is completed. After the retreat a detailed summary is provided.

Retreat Location

The Center for Career and Business Development in North Eastham, Massachusetts, in close proximity to the Cape Cod National Seashore, which features over sixty miles of undeveloped beach beneath an all-encompassing sky. Accommodations are available nearby at a discounted rate.

For more information, visit:
www.SuccessOnYourOwnTerms.com/careerretreats.htm
or send an email to: info@SuccessOnYourOwnTerms.com.

•

"What an enlightened way to spend a day. Imagine talking about my professional life with such candor and connectedness. I believe you and your space are magic."

"I appreciate your can-do, upbeat, positive thinking approach. It is no wonder that you have coached so many people to success. I also value your recognition that everyone must build their career to their own specifications and there's no one-size-fits-all methodology."

Bibliography

Alboher, Marci, *One Person, Multiple Careers*, New York: Warner Business Books, 2007

Bennis, Warren, and Joan Goldsmith, *Learning to Lead*, Cambridge, MA: Perseus Books, 1997

Bolles, Richard N., *The Three Boxes of Life*, Berkeley: Ten Speed Press, 1978

— ,*What Color Is Your Parachute?*, Berkeley: Ten Speed Press, 2002

Bridges, William, *Creating You & Co.*, Reading, MA: Perseus Books, 1997

—, *Jobshift*, Reading, MA: Addison-Wesley Publishing Co., 1994

—, *Managing Transition: Making the Most of Change*, Reading, MA: Addison-Wesley Publishing Co., 1991

—, *Surviving Corporate Transition*, Mill Valley, CA: William Bridges and Associates, 1988

—, *The Way of Transition*, Cambridge, MA: Perseus Publishing, 2001

—, *Transitions: Making Sense of Life's Changes*, Reading, MA: Addison-Wesley Publishing Co., 1980

Cloke, Kenneth, and Joan Goldsmith, *The Art of Waking People Up: Cultivating Awareness and Authenticity at Work*, San Francisco: Jossey-Bass, 2003

Dent, Harry S. Jr., *The Great Jobs Ahead*, New York: Hyperion, 1995

Drucker, Peter F., *Management Challenges for the 21st Century*, New York: Harper Collins, 1991

—, *The Essential Drucker,* New York: Harper Collins, 2001

Ehrenreich, Barbara, *Bait and Switch: The (Futile) Pursuit of the American Dream,* New York: Metropolitan Books, 2005

Gerber, Michael, *The E-Myth Revisited,* New York: Harper Collins, 1995

Hakim, Cliff, *We Are All Self-Employed,* San Francisco: Barrett-Coehler Publishers, Inc., 2003

Lassiter, Pam, *The New Job Security,* Berkeley: Ten Speed Press, 2002

Lindbergh, Anne Morrow, *Gift from the Sea,* New York: Random House, 1955

Pink, Daniel, *Free Agent Nation,* New York: Business Plus, 2002

Rogers, Carl, *A Way of Being,* New York: Houghton-Mifflin, 1980

Schramm, Carl J., *The Entrepreneurial Imperative,* New York: Harper Collins, 2006

Taylor, Jeff, and Doug Hardy, *Monster Careers,* New York: Penguin Books, 2004

Wheatley, Margaret J., *Leadership and the New Science,* San Francisco: Barrett-Coehler Publishers, Inc., 1991

Wheatley, Margaret J., *Finding Our Way,* San Francisco: Barrett-Coehler Publishers, Inc., 2005

Whyte, David, *Crossing the Unknown Sea: Work As a Pilgrimage of Identity,* New York: Riverhead Books, 2001

Zander, Rosamund Stone, and Benjamin Zander, *The Art of Possibility,* New York: Penguin Books, 2002

Index

Acknowledgements

A few years ago, when I was thinking about all the reasons why I could not write this book—elderly parents, a demanding work schedule, eleven grandchildren—and making a case for not doing it, another thought slipped sideways into my mind. I had everyone I needed to help me accomplish the goal. My husband Michael is a excellent writer and editor. Joan Goldsmith, my mentor and writing teacher, would help me get started. My dear friend, Eloise Morley would provide both her wonderful illustrations and gentle encouragement. Gillian Drake would publish it and by her very participation add grace to the project. As the faces of this core circle emerged from the communities I inhabit, the haze of my self-doubt began to clear. In addition to those mentioned above, career professionals and more experienced writers too numerous to name have blessed me with their interest in my ideas and offered constructive suggestions. I am also grateful to friends like Tina, Angela, Sherri, Kyle, Jane, Barbara, and Hilda, who have kept me in touch with the greater purpose of my effort. Finally, I am indebted to my clients, who boldly step forward, trusting in the process, and allow me to participate in their professional growth.